God's Redemption for All

God's Redemption for All

Being One in Christ

Bishop Audrey Drummonds, PH.D.

*Living as God's Kings and
Priest on the Earth Today*

authorHOUSE®

AuthorHouse™
1663 Liberty Drive
Bloomington, IN 47403
www.authorhouse.com
Phone: 833-262-8899

Unless otherwise noted in the text, all Scriptures have been taken from the King James Version Hebrew-Greek Key Study Bible copyright 1984 and 1991 Sprios Zodhiate and AMG International, Inc. D/B/A/ Amg Publishers

Scripture taken from THE AMPLIFIED BIBLE, Old Testament copyright 1965, 1987 by the Zondervan Corporation. The Amplified New Testament copyright 1958, 1987 by the Lockman Foundation.

Scripture taken from The Message. Copyright © 1993, 1994, 1995, 1996, 2000, 2001, 2002. Used by permission of NavPress Publishing Group."

Published by AuthorHouse 09/29/2021

ISBN: 978-1-5049-5777-9 (sc)
ISBN: 978-1-5049-5776-2 (e)

Print information available on the last page.

Any people depicted in stock imagery provided by Thinkstock are models, and such images are being used for illustrative purposes only. Certain stock imagery © Thinkstock.

This book is printed on acid-free paper.

Because of the dynamic nature of the Internet, any web addresses or links contained in this book may have changed since publication and may no longer be valid. The views expressed in this work are solely those of the author and do not necessarily reflect the views of the publisher, and the publisher hereby disclaims any responsibility for them.

Other books by Bishop Audrey Drummonds, PH.D.

Bringing Forth the Sons of God

The Book of Revelation (Vol 1); Christ in You, the Hope of Glory

The Book of Revelation (Vol. 2) Chapters 8-13

Living in the Inheritance of God

Rising to Royalty

Prelude

Proverbs 8
(The Message)

Lady Wisdom Calls Out

Do you hear Lady Wisdom calling? Can you hear Madame Insight
raising her voice?
She's taken her stand at First and Main,
at the busiest intersection.
Right in the city square
where the traffic is thickest, she shouts,
"You—I'm talking to all of you,
everyone out here on the streets!
Listen, you idiots—learn good sense!
You blockheads—shape up!
Don't miss a word of this—I'm telling you how to live well,
I'm telling you how to live at your best.
My mouth chews and savors and relishes truth—
I can't stand the taste of evil!
You'll only hear true and right words from my mouth;

not one syllable will be twisted or skewed.
You'll recognize this as true—you with open minds;
truth-ready minds will see it at once.
Prefer my life-disciplines over chasing after money,
and God-knowledge over a lucrative career.
For Wisdom is better than all the trappings of wealth;
nothing you could wish for holds a candle to her.

"I am Lady Wisdom, and I live next to Sanity;
Knowledge and Discretion live just down the street.
The Fear-of-God means hating Evil,
whose ways I hate with a passion—
pride and arrogance and crooked talk.
Good counsel and common sense are my characteristics;
I am both Insight and the Virtue to live it out.
With my help, leaders rule,
and lawmakers legislate fairly;
With my help, governors govern,
along with all in legitimate authority.
I love those who love me;
those who look for me find me.
Wealth and Glory accompany me—
also substantial Honor and a Good Name.
My benefits are worth more than a big salary, even a very big salary;
the returns on me exceed any imaginable bonus.
You can find me on Righteous Road—that's where I walk—
at the intersection of Justice Avenue,
Handing out life to those who love me,
filling their arms with life—armloads of life!"

"God sovereignly made me—the first, the basic—
before he did anything else.
I was brought into being a long time ago,
well before Earth got its start.

I arrived on the scene before Ocean,
yes, even before Springs and Rivers and Lakes.
Before Mountains were sculpted and Hills took shape,
I was already there, newborn;
Long before God stretched out Earth's Horizons,
and tended to the minute details of Soil and Weather,
And set Sky firmly in place,
I was there.
When he mapped and gave borders to wild Ocean,
built the vast vault of Heaven,
and installed the fountains that fed Ocean,
When he drew a boundary for Sea,
posted a sign that said no trespassing,
And then staked out Earth's Foundations,
I was right there with him, making sure everything fit.
Day after day I was there, with my joyful applause,
always enjoying his company,
Delighted with the world of things and creatures,
happily celebrating the human family."

"So, my dear friends, listen carefully;
those who embrace these my ways are most blessed.
Mark a life of discipline and live wisely;
don't squander your precious life.
Blessed the man, blessed the woman, who listens to me,
awake and ready for me each morning,
alert and responsive as I start my day's work.
When you find me, you find life, real life,
to say nothing of God's good pleasure.
But if you wrong me, you damage your very soul;
when you reject me, you're flirting with death."

The Message (MSG) by Eugene H. Peterson
Scripture taken from *The Message*. Copyright © 1993, 1994, 1995, 1996, 2000, 2001, 2002. Used by permission of NavPress Publishing Group.

Contents

Author's Notes

Psalm 45

"You are the most excellent of men.
Your lips have been given the ability to speak gracious words.
God has blessed you forever.
Mighty one, put your sword at your side.
Put on glory and majesty as if they were your clothes.
In your majesty ride out with power
in honor of what is true and right.
Do it in honor of all those who are not proud.
Let your right hand do wonderful things.
Shoot your sharp arrows into the hearts of your enemies.
Let the nations come under your control.
Your throne is the very throne of God.
Your kingdom will last forever and ever.

(Psalm 45: 2-6. New International Reader's Version (NIRV) Copyright © 1996, 1998
by International Bible Society)

When we allow ourselves to stay under the training of others, becoming complacent to what the Holy Spirit has revealed to them, our relationship with God becomes second hand leaving us in a childlike state of expectancy. To be able to BE the manifested Sons of God requires having a relationship with God based on one's personal experience, and not allowing someone else to do the pursuing of knowing God as Father for you. One of the difficulties of being a teacher is when people become co-dependent upon the teacher instead of searching out a relationship with God for himself or herself.

God will eagerly show each of us His unique revelation from the manifold wisdom of our individual understanding. However, if we follow the teaching of an individual (pastor, professor), then we only have a relationship with God as seen in the teacher's portion of God's revelation, and we end up being a copy of the teacher. If we are going to be empowered to know Him for ourselves there must be an experience in God that is unique to each individual.

The teacher's job is to share their experience and understanding to provoke the student to go beyond the teacher and search out the revelation of God that is unique to their part of the body of Christ that will bring together humanity as one body in Christ. God will use the circumstances, failures and successes, of each individual's life to bring about His conclusions. It may not seem so while we go through circumstances in our life, but when we look back, we can see the bigger picture of why God led us through the paths we traveled.

If a student always dependent upon the teacher, then the student will only know the secrets of God through subliminal messages of what the teacher says. For example: If the teacher says, "God is going to bless you or heal you," and you affirm that with "Amen," then subliminally, you have given place to an atmosphere that at the moment you are not blessed or healed. This mindset holds the student in bondage of ever seeking the blessing or healing; never quite obtaining the fullness of their inheritance that is available for today.

Once we fall into the trap of bondage, we bring life through our creative imagination that poverty, sickness, and death exist. However, with God, everything is not "going to be" someday, but already IS. It is not something He is going to do, but has already been completed in Him. The objective of the student is to mature in Christ moving into the role of teacher and sharing their portion of Christ to others.

The chapters in this book are a collection of teachings the Holy Spirit has shared with the author. You will find the writings are not in accordance to proper grammar, but have been shared within the pattern the Holy Spirit taught. Some of the wisdom you will find to be profound, full of an in-depth love of God that goes beyond comprehension. Other writings will be confusing and difficult to understand. In such cases, these interpretations will be a portion of revelation the Holy Spirit has given the author that the reader is not ready to receive...yet. It is at these moments it is suggested to the reader proceed with caution not allowing logic and reason to try to comprehend wisdom that only the Holy Spirit can reveal. Instead, consider opening your mind to a teachable spirit. Clear past comprehension taught by various doctrines or denominations, and allow the Holy Spirit to surround the reader with His peace and love.

From this perspective, the student will fine all the treasures of wisdom hid in Christ. God will begin to charge the reader with the power of an endless life after the order of Melchizedek ruling and reigning as kings and priests on the earth.

The teachings in this book have been compiled from essays written for our website, www.ICMinistry.org. The website offers a wonderful opportunity to reach people around the world with the Good News of the Gospel of Jesus Christ. However, without a hard copy of the material, it is difficult for the reader to ponder the teachings and/or do an in-depth study. We have therefore put some of the teachings into book form. All proceeds received from the sale of this book are given to Interior Coverings Ministry, a nonprofit organization since 2002, to be used for outreach missions furthering the Kingdom of God. I encourage the use of highlighters, underlining, and note taking in the margins as the Holy Spirit stirs your inner being. At the end of each chapter are pages to do personal reflection and meditation. Ask the Holy Spirit to show you something new that you didn't see before.

"Because of the LORD's great love we are not consumed,
for his compassions never fail. They are new every morning;
great is your faithfulness. I say to myself, "The LORD is my portion;
therefore I will wait for him."
Lamentations 3:22-24 (NIV)

Father,

In Jesus name, we have been tried, and we have conquered, breaking the patterns of mindsets full of evil and darkness. The strongholds that have challenged us in the past have caused us to come through the fires of hell with the overcoming victory that death has been defeated, and today we have the ability to know the power of His resurrected Life.

Father, you have come, invading and riding as a majestic King in the hearts and minds of your people; ruling Christ in the hearts of men; purifying and cleansing with the promise of victory; conquering and to conquer causing flames of fire for purification bringing what has been dead in the earth to life; and that which has been silent to be heard through the voice of your sons in knowledge and understanding.

You Father, have prepared the book that was sealed. You have released the Christ who is worthy to break the seals and open the book. Let us come now as one body in Christ Jesus saying, "Lo, I come (in the volume of the book it is written of me,) to do thy will, O God" (Hebrews 10:7).

Amen

Introduction

The secrets of God can only be given to those He has chosen by His sovereign grace, to not only take others to the steps of His Holy Temple, but also to bring them into His Holy presence. These people must have an inward pursuit of not only hearing the word, but also **being** the word, or the vessel, that Christ can flow through for others to be blessed by the presence of their Father's Holiness while in their natural body.

In Isaiah 11, the prophet shares that the Holy Spirit is manifested in fullness when the 7-fold spirits of God come into full maturity. This is not seven different spirits, but parts of the same Spirit that edify, equip, and enhance one another.

"And there shall come forth a rod out of the stem of Jesse, and a Branch shall grow out of his roots: And the spirit of the LORD shall rest upon him, the spirit of wisdom and understanding, the spirit of counsel and might, the spirit of knowledge and of the fear of the LORD; And shall make him of quick understanding in the fear of the LORD: and he shall not judge after the sight of his eyes, neither reprove after the hearing of his ears: But with righteousness shall he judge the poor, and reprove with equity for the meek

of the earth: and he shall smite the earth with the rod of his mouth, and with the breath of his lips shall he slay the wicked" (Isaiah 11:1-4).

Moses did not read Genesis, but wrote it by what the Holy Spirit revealed to him. The Proverbs given to us by Solomon came from the Spirit of Wisdom documented by what Moses wrote (Proverbs 8:23).

King Solomon emphasized that we must first obtain the "Spirit of Wisdom" in order to be able to obtain the Spirit of God in counsel, might, knowledge, fear of the Lord, and righteous judgment.

"Get wisdom, get understanding: forget it not; neither decline from the words of my mouth. Forsake her not, and she shall preserve thee: love her, and she shall keep thee. Wisdom is the principal thing; therefore get wisdom: and with all thy getting get understanding. Exalt her, and she shall promote thee: she shall bring thee to honor, when thou dost embrace her. She shall give to thine head an ornament of grace: a crown of glory shall she deliver to thee" (Proverbs 4:5-9).

Today, we have the ability to read the wisdom that Moses was given to write. We have the blessing to discern the Spirit of Wisdom by what Solomon saw. However, for us to receive the Spirit of Wisdom for our own life we must allow the faith of God to impregnate His vision and understanding that goes beyond our perception that Moses and Solomon have shared.

Paul had been raised with the teachings of the Old Testament and interpretations of Moses, Isaiah, and Solomon according to the law. When Jesus confronted him that he had been persecuting God instead of glorifying Him, Paul zealously ventured across cities, territories, and nations to preach Christ. Paul taught that the Gospel of Jesus Christ was more than just knowing God after the law; but also as Father. He writes to the Colossians, *"That their hearts might be comforted, being knit together in love, and unto all riches of the full assurance of understanding, to the acknowledgement of the mystery of*

God, and of the Father, and of Christ; In whom are hid all the treasures of wisdom and knowledge" (Colassians 2:2-3).

Paul shares with the Corinthians, *"Where is the wise man? Where is the scholar? Where is the philosopher of this age? Has not God made foolish the wisdom of the world? For since in the wisdom of God the world through its wisdom did not know him, God was pleased through the foolishness of what was preached to save those who believe. Jews demand miraculous signs and Greeks look for wisdom, but we preach Christ crucified: a stumbling block to Jews and foolishness to Gentiles, but to those whom God has called, both Jews and Greeks, Christ the power of God and the wisdom of God. For the foolishness of God is wiser than man's wisdom, and the weakness of God is stronger than man's strength"* (1 Corinthians 1:20-25, NIV).

The Spirit of Wisdom was released "in the beginning" by anointing Moses to write Genesis. She gave voice to the patriarchs and prophets with types and shadows of the ways of God in the Old Testament. She opened the eyes of the disciples to know God as Father in the New Testament. She gave heavenly understanding to earthly application to Paul. With this journey through the Scriptures the revelation of Christ in you, the hope of glory, has been declared for humanity to reign as sons of God. *"As He is, so are we in this world"* (1 John 4:17). Let us enter into the Kingdom of God…

God uses the Spirit of Wisdom to build His house and cut out of her seven pillars (Proverbs 9:1). In Exodus 31, God gave the Spirit of Wisdom to one man to build the Tabernacle of God and all that was in it during the times of Moses. He didn't choose Moses or Aaron to build it, but entrusted His house with a man that dwelled in the shadow of the secret place of the Most High named Bezalel (Psalms 91:1).

Receiving the Spirit of Wisdom from God is not a "Santa Claus" issue where we ask for wisdom and God gives it to spoiled children. The Spirit of God must be known through "Passover," "Pentecost," and "Tabernacle" journeys. God does not forsake us, but gives us opportunities to grow and mature in Christ by the trials of our faith developing patience. Patience will bring about a finished maturity causing us to want or lack nothing (James 1:2-5). If we are lacking wisdom, God will cause the trials of our faith to be released to develop patience. The Wisdom of God will kill all the beast of our carnal understanding (Proverbs 9:2).

The teachings in this book are a collection of Wisdom revealed by the Holy Spirit to show us our Heavenly Father through Jesus Christ. We are told to, "*study to show thyself approved unto God, a workman that needeth not to be ashamed, rightly dividing the word of truth*" (2 Timothy 2:15), that the voice of our hearts may shout in one Spirit, "*Holy, holy, holy, is the LORD of hosts: the whole earth is full of his glory*" (Isaiah 6:3).

CHAPTER 1

Free Will or Heavenly Mind

1 Corinthians 15 AMP

If we do not understand what it means to be heavenly minded, we would find ourselves falling back in a trap of our own will and desire to obtain a goal believing that we are pleasing God. Whether that goal is to have a personal relationship with God or natural achievements, we will stay ensnared with our own self-efforts and works that can never be good enough no matter how hard we try.

Verse 45-49:

"Thus it is written, the first man Adam became a living being (an individual personality); *the last Adam* (Christ) *became a life-giving Spirit* (restoring the dead to life (Gen. 2:7). *But it is not the spiritual life which came first, but the physical and then the spiritual. The first man* (was) *from out of earth, made of dust* (earthly-minded); *the second Man* (is) *the Lord from out of heaven. Not those who are made of the dust are like him who was first made of the dust* (earthly-minded); *and as is* (the Man) *from heaven, so also* (are those) *who are of heaven* (heavenly-minded). *And just as we have borne the image* (of the man) *of dust, so shall we and so let us also bear the image* (of the Man) *of heaven."*

The first Adam focused on himself (earth-minded); the second Adam focused on a corporate body (heavenly-minded). Once baptism into Christ occurs, we lose our individual personality and become corporate minded as one body. Being heavenly minded is not about acknowledging a personal relationship with God, but accepting a corporate identity of being one in Christ. This means that our individual identity becomes dependent on the rest of the body of Christ by which we function as one body.

This sounds good until we find ourselves wanting others to conform to what we consider a righteous Christian. We can no longer declare ourselves to be a Christian in the eyes of God while establishing a mindset filled with judgment and condemnation on others because they have not acknowledge Jesus as their Lord and Savior.

The Heavenly minded soul searches the heart of the Father asking the Holy Spirit, "How would Jesus respond to this? What would He do?"

Theology or a title referred to as being a Christian does not establish the body of Christ. Paul tells us that we are a many member body, but yet one Christ with Jesus as the head of the body. Being a Christian is freedom from the individual personality and identity as one person, and coming into a corporate unity as one in Him. A finger or toe cannot function individually. They must be attached to the hand or foot, which also requires connections with the arms or legs, etc. etc.

Galatians 2:20

"I have been crucified with Christ (in Him I have shared His crucifixion); *it is no longer I who live, but Christ* (the Messiah) *lives in me; and the life I now live in the body I live by faith in* (by adherence to and reliance on and complete trust in) *the Son of God, who loved me and gave Himself up for me."*

As Christians, we are no longer an individual earthly body or personality looking out for ourselves, but a part of the physical, tangible, natural body of Christ which is depended on the rest of the body to function as one.

To be heavenly minded requires us to understand the one that rules the body by being submissive to the mind of Jesus Christ. We must first understand what the second Adam was like that was different from the first. A key element in understanding the mind of Jesus Christ is to realize that God does not change; He is consistently the same throughout time. He is not subject to change in His Being or attributes. The permanence of God's character guarantees the fulfillment of His promises.

The unchanging ability of God is our assurance that God's promises are already finished. Before time began, His promises were already completed. The consistency of His Being allows us to function by faith that His promises will be manifested according to His will, and not by anything that we do. God knows all that was going to happen before it happened. If the promises of God were dependent on our will, then there is a high probability that they would not happen. It would mean that the will of man is greater than the promises of God.

Since God has no beginning and no end, He can know no change. He does not evolve, grow, improve, or deteriorate. He is not dependent on the will of humanity. He is already perfect. James 1:17-18 tells us, *"Every good gift and every perfect* (free, large, full) *gift is from above; it comes down from the Father of all* (that gives) *light, in* (the shining of) *whom there can be no variation* (rising or setting) *or shadow cast by His turning* (as in an eclipse). *And it was of His own* (free) *will that He gave us birth* (as sons) *by* (His) *Word of Truth, so that we should be a kind of fistfights of His creatures* (a sample of what He created to be consecrated to Himself)."

Regardless of how individually we relate to God, He is consistently the same. There are no shadows of negativism, darkness, condemnation, judgment, limitations, or any conditions that could cause us to be able to change God. He is unconditional LOVE, LIGHT, and ETERNAL LIFE. In Him, there is no darkness in any form (1 John 1:5).

"For I am the Lord, I do not change; that is why you, O sons of Jacob, are not consumed"
Malachi3:6

Not only does God not change, but He also does not react, or move by our thoughts or actions. He already knows the end from the beginning. Therefore, whether we sin or act righteous; whether we beg and plead or rebel in self-defiance, we cannot cause God to change or respond any different from His identity and character of unconditional love. The only things that can change are either we draw closer to God or we draw ourselves away from God based on our own deeds, actions, and thoughts. Our relationship with God is reflected by the choices we make. God does not change, and neither does our identity as His children based on His will.

God sees us in the beloved son-ship of Jesus Christ. He sees us as His body. God does not see us in time, but eternity of what is already finished. Ecclesiastes 3:14-15, *"I know that whatever God does, it endures forever; nothing can be added to it nor anything taken from it. And God does it so that men will* (reverently) *fear Him* (revere and worship Him, knowing that He is). *That which is now already has been, and that which is to be already has been; and God seeks that which has passed by* (so that history repeats itself)."

That which has been is NOW. That which is going to be has already been. What you are going through in life has already been in God. What we experiencing today has already been accomplished. Therefore, what has been in God is NOW being manifested in us. All that God is doing is already finished. There is no way around God.

Isaiah 46: 10 says, *"Declaring the end and the result from the beginning, and from ancient times the things that are not yet done, saying, My counsel shall stand, and I will do all My pleasure and purpose."* 2 Corinthians 4:15, *"For all* (these) *things are* (taking place) *for your sake, so that the more grace* (divine favor and spiritual blessing) *extends to more and more people and multiplies through the many, the more thanksgiving may increase* (and redound) *to the glory of God."*

The Lamb was slain before the foundation of the world. Every good deed or bad behavior that we may experience is not being ignored by God, but has already been crucified at Calvary over 2000 years ago. God is declaring this to us. Everything in Christ is what He sees in us. Our debt with sin outside of Christ has been paid. This is the grace of God. He is not bringing us into a realm of righteousness, but unveiling the fact that we already are in Him.

What does God gain or lose if we are good or bad? In Job 35:6-7 we read, *"If you have sinned, how does that affect God? And if your transgressions are multiplied, what have you done to Him? If you are righteous, what do you* (by that) *give God? Or what does He receive from you hand?"* Our actions cannot change God at all because He is consistently the same. As for us, it is in Him we live and move and have our being (Acts 17:28).

What does man's "free-will" mean from God perception?

With this in mind, we address the issue of what the body of Christ has been taught concerning "the free will of man." Religion teaches that every person has the ability to "will" the refusal of God and spend eternity in hell, or the "will" to choose Him through Jesus Christ as his or her personal savior. If this were true, then man has more power than the will of God. However, knowing that this is not true, we must re-evaluate the "will of mankind" by being heavenly minded versus listening to our earthly understanding.

Romans 12:3 says, *"For by the grace given to me I warn everyone among you not to estimate and think of himself more highly than he ought* (not to have an exaggerated opinion of his own importance), *but to rate his ability with sober judgment, each according to the degree of faith apportioned by God to him. For as in one physical body we have many parts* (organs, members) *and all of these parts do not have the same function or use, so we, numerous as we are, are one body in Christ* (the Messiah) *and individually we are parts one of another* (mutually dependent on one another.)"

How often do we hear Christians say that they are saved and going to heaven? Then from the same person, there will be separation of the body to the body of Christ because they consider that others are not? Judgment comes because of what believers see outwardly instead of searching the hearts of people. A major reason that there are non-believers is because of the mindset of the believers boasting of themselves while judging others. Our words have the ability to create life or death in the atmosphere around us.

Our created purpose is to unite the body of Christ as one body in Him. We are the manifestation of Him. Since God can only have a relationship with Himself, we cannot separate some people and include others in our thoughts and actions towards one another. Jesus came to this earth to gather people to Himself and connect all humanity as one body. If we place judgment on someone else to be a sinner, we cannot consider ourselves sinless. If we declare ourselves a Christian, we must see all humankind through the eyes of God as already righteous even though they themselves may not acknowledge this truth.

The greatest faith we manifest is His faith within us believing that the whole earth is filled with the glory of God. Our natural mind cannot comprehend this. It must come by the faith of God given to each of us by His grace and activated by His unconditional love, which is our identity in Him. When we get hold of the reality of who our Heavenly Father is, we then can walk in the manifestation of as He is, so are we in this world (1 John 4:17).

When we exalt ourselves, while judging others, we come against God. It would be like us trying to function in our natural body with our arms making demands to do one thing and our feet stubbornly going in a different direction. At the same time, our heart is beating irregularly; our stomach is up chucking its contents; our intestines are gurgling and expelling its matter; and our kidneys and liver have decided to stop working. Can we really believe if our natural body was trying to go through a day in this kind of condition that our mind would be full of unconditional love, peace, and harmony? Yet, this is an example of how we try to function as the body of Christ splitting ourselves apart because of doctrines, theologies, and opinions of what WE THINK God means with scripture.

It is not possible to be a non-judgmental, non-critical person on our own. We need the connection of one another to cover each other with His love, mercy, and forgiveness that we each have with us. The natural disasters occurring around the world speak to our identity as sons of God to be apparent. We put aside our opinions, politics, religions, and race opening our hearts to those in need. Why do we do this? Because it is the unconditional love of the Father in us which is our identity being lifted up drawing all men unto Him (John 12:32).

"I assure you, most solemnly I tell you, unless a grain of wheat falls into the earth and dies, it remains (just one grain; it never becomes more but lives) *by itself alone. But if it dies, it produces many others and yields a rich harvest"* (John 12:24).

"I have been crucified with Christ (in Him I have shared His crucifixion); *it is no longer I* (self, individual, first Adam) *who live, but Christ* (the Messiah, last Adam) *lives in me; and the life I now live in the body* (corporately in Christ) *I live by faith* (given by God) *in* (by adherence

to and reliance on and complete trust in) *the Son of God, who loved me and gave Himself up for me"* (Galatians 2:20).

> *"The Lord possessed me in the beginning of his way, before his works of old. I was set up from everlasting, from the beginning, or ever the earth was. When there were no depths, I was brought forth; when there were no fountains abounding with water, before the mountains were settled, before the hills was I brought forth; while as yet he had not made the earth, nor the fields, nor the highest part of the dust of the world. When he prepared the heavens, I was there; When he set a compass upon the face of the depth; when he established the clouds above; when he strengthened the fountains of the deep; when he gave to the sea his decree, that the waters should not pass his commandment; when he appointed the foundations of the earth: Then I was by him, as one brought up with him; and I was daily his delight, rejoicing always before him; rejoicing in the habitable part of his earth; and my delights were with the sons of men"* (Proverbs 8:22-31).

We have the opportunity to make free-will choices in heavenly minded decisions in the earth while in our natural body. Jesus Christ gave this access to the Father by His Grace, dunamis power, when we received Jesus as our Lord and the begotten Son of God. This free will comes in the realm of our sowing and reaping that grace umbrellas. Father's teachings and instructions in His Torah which was used for Jesus and Paul have not changed. They still instruct us to live on the earth knowing the difference between clean and unclean, Holy and unholy through the practices of the feast days of the Lord called the moedims. Jesus did away with the law of sin and death, but not the instructions and teachings of the Father.

When we do the Father's teachings we bring Heaven into our atmosphere in the earth. 1Peter 2:9, he stated to believers in Christ

Jesus that they were a peculiarly people of royal priesthood, a Holy nation. As such we have a responsibility to be a witness of Jesus Christ by, *"teaching my people the difference between the holy and the common and show them how to distinguish between the unclean and the clean. In any dispute, the priests are to serve as judges and decide it according to my ordinances. They are to keep my laws and my decrees for all my appointed festivals, and they are to keep my Sabbaths holy."* Ezekiel 44:22-24.

Notes of reflection and meditation

What were your immediate thoughts as you read this chapter?

_____

_____

_____

_____

_____

_____

What seemed confusing from what you thought?

_____

_____

_____

_____

_____

_____

What was something new that you had not heard before?

_____

_____

_____

_____

_____

_____

CHAPTER 2

It is Time...Awake

A key to help us in understanding the Bible can be found in the book of Genesis, the first 3 verses of chapter one:

- **Gen. 1:1** God is present, but there is no spoken word.
- **Gen. 1:2** There is the movement upon the water (the word) because we need the word of God.
- **Gen. 1:3** "God said." We now have the spoken word of God which is "Let there be Light" or let there be ME.

God's whole plan for this earth is that it would be full of His glory, or His sons. The 'glory' is the character and nature of the parent seen in the children. I have purposely highlighted many Bible passages including bold words. Please do not skip over these Scriptures out of familiarity, but meditate asking the Holy Spirit to unveil the wisdom of the Father that you did not know before.

Haggai 2:7

*"I will shake **all** nations* (people), *and the desire of **all** nations* (people) *shall come: and I will fill this house* (people) *with glory* (character and nature of Himself), *saith the LORD of hosts."*

God will fill His house, which is our natural body, with Himself. He is talking to us as the host of the house or our identity in Him. Gen 2:1, *"Thus the heavens and the earth were finished, and **the entire** host* (sons of God) *of them."* The host is the "Lights" or the sons of God.

The pattern in Genesis 1 is darkness before light. The Spirit of God moves to bring forth His word or Himself. This word from God is always Light because He is Light. God cannot speak darkness or anything contrary to His identity. Some people consider the Light of God as revelation knowledge. In times past, we have been trying to know about God with our own knowledge or intellect. A major difference between the two is that revelation knowledge can never be changed or taken from us, but our own understanding changes according to the experience we have.

Now, stay with me as we look at an illustration of how God operates. In the natural when nighttime approaches and darkness falls around us, our bodies tend is to slow down and go to sleep. When Scripture refers to being asleep it is an illustration of being ignorant to the understanding of God (whether one is alive in their natural body or dead in the grave). Before Jesus Christ came to this earth, people were in darkness or asleep. They may have been awake in the natural, but they were asleep to the revelation knowledge of God that would awaken them spiritually. Jesus was the first STAR that brought LIGHT to the world awakening the people of God from the darkness they were in. Before Christ came to the earth, humankind was likened to a hidden star sitting in darkness.

Luke 9:7-8

"Now Herod the tetrarch heard of all that was done by him: and he was perplexed, because that it was said of some, that John was risen from the dead; And of some, that Elias had appeared; and of others, that one of the old prophets was risen again." The issue here is that the king was upset

because he believed there was the possibility that someone who was dead could come back to life and threaten his kingdom. This belief was so strong that he demanded genocide of all the male children two years old and under. Was he wrong to believe someone who resurrected from the grave would threaten his position and authority?

Luke 9:27-36

"But I tell you of a truth, there be some standing here, which shall not taste of death, till they see the kingdom of God. And it came to pass about eight days (spiritual new beginning) *after these sayings, he took Peter and John and James, and went up into a mountain to pray. And as he prayed, the fashion of his countenance was altered, and his raiment* (outer garment) *was white and glistering* (surrounded by darkness). *And, behold, there talked with him two men, which were Moses and Elias* (came forth out of the darkness of ignorance): *Who appeared in glory, and spoke of his decease which he should accomplish at Jerusalem. But Peter and they that were with him were heavy with sleep* (ignorant of spiritual understanding): *and when they were awake, they saw his glory, and the two men that stood with him. And it came to pass, as they departed from him, Peter said unto Jesus, Master, it is good for us to be here: and let us make three tabernacles* (kingdoms); *one for thee, and one for Moses, and one for Elias: not knowing what he said. While he thus spoke, there came a cloud* (glory, character and nature of God), *and overshadowed them: and they feared as they entered into the cloud. And there came a voice out of the cloud, saying, this is my beloved Son: hear him. And when the voice was past, Jesus was found alone* (there is only one Christ). *And they kept it close, and told no man in those days any of those things which they had seen."*

Moses understood something about the glory of God. In. Exodus 33:18, *"And he said, I beseech thee, shew me thy glory."* Moses knew that when revelation knowledge comes upon you and His glory fills you; you become His glory. This glory cannot be changed.

Now, let us get a picture of what was going on. Jesus goes to the mountain of transformation to talk with Moses and Elias about his decease. We do not actually know what the conversation was, but "his decease" could have been about the death, burial, and resurrection of Jesus Christ. However, it could have also included the transformation of the body of Christ that would take place which would include Moses, Elijah, and all those in the graves which were opened at the time Jesus hung on the cross and the veil into the Holy of Holies was torn apart (Matthew 27: 49-53). Peter, James, and John are witnesses to the Light in the midst of darkness and they see the transformation. Scripture does not tell us what time of day Jesus went to the mount of transformation, but it does tell us that the Light caused transformation of Jesus' raiment or how they saw him. Interesting, while this was going on the disciples were heavy with sleep. When they tried to grasp what just took place with their natural understanding, God immediately had corrected them revealing that there was only one Christ even though they saw Jesus and two men.

Later, Jesus took the same three men to the Garden of Gethsemane, which was called the "wine press," telling them to stay awake and watch. They missed the full understanding of what took place at the mount of transformation because they fell asleep. You would think that this time when the master told them to stay awake they would have done everything in their power not to miss what Jesus wanted them to see.

Mark 14:33-41

"And he taketh with him Peter and James and John, and began to be sore amazed and to be very heavy; and saith unto them, my soul is exceeding sorrowful unto death: tarry ye here, and watch. And he went forward a little, and fell on the ground, and prayed that, if it were possible, the hour might pass from him. And he said, Abba, Father, all things are possible unto thee; take away this cup from me: nevertheless not what I will, but

what thou wilt. And he cometh, and findeth them sleeping, and saith unto Peter, Simon, sleepest thou? Couldest not thou watch one hour? Watch ye and pray, lest ye enter into temptation. The spirit truly is ready, but the flesh is weak. And again he went away, and prayed, and spake the same words. And when he returned, he found them asleep again, (for their eyes were heavy,) neither wist they what to answer him. And he cometh the third time, and saith unto them, Sleep on now, and take your rest: it is enough, the hour is come; behold, the Son of man is betrayed into the hands of sinners."

Jesus had taken the same three men who witnessed the transformed life of Moses and Elijah just prior to his moment of dealing with his death in Gethsemane. During the covenant exchange of Passover, Jesus took the sin of natural man. He was the Light, but the Light had gone out, and He was in total darkness. He needed the covering of love for what He was going through. Jesus was not asking these men to just naturally stay awake, but spiritually be awake. *"The spirit is willing, but the flesh is weak."*

Jesus was not condemning the disciples, but expressing history of what was written for us today, and every generation throughout time. It is God who reveals Himself. Both of these scenes are for our benefit: to understand that God is here today in our midst even though we cannot see Him; to understand that no matter how much we may desire to please God with our natural mind, we will fail every time. It

Ritual baths, called Mikveh, were common during the time of Jesus. They were a part of spiritual cleansing, not physical in order to enter the presence of God. When one went into the waters, and then emerged, they were pronounced "Born Again!" This was a life style, not a one-time baptism.

was God's will for Jesus to endure all that He went through in the garden and the cross. If the disciples had intervened in any way trying to be noble for the Lord, it would have affected all humanity.

The agony of sin can bring overwhelming levels of inner pain and turmoil. It takes the love of God to cleanse us from it. This agony may not be experienced immediately or publicly, but it will eventually appear; especially when sin (ignorance or darkness) are confronted with the presence of those that are walking as Jesus did. People that do not know the Father's love must experience it by the sons of God on the earth. We may be the only love from heaven a person may connect with which is why we must be the manifestation of "no condemnation."

Jesus became the darkness of sin. Sin is darkness. The fullness of Adam's sin was his disbelief in God's will. God did not give us a choice to believe Him. God commanded that we believe by faith, and He gave each of us a measure of His faith to make it possible.

Something that is missed often when reading Luke 9 regarding the mount of transfiguration can be found in verses 34-36:

"While he thus spake, there came a cloud, and overshadowed them: and they feared as they entered into the cloud. And there came a voice out of the cloud, saying, this is my beloved Son: hear him. And when the voice was past, Jesus was found alone. And they kept it close, and told no man in those days any of those things which they had seen."

While Peter was speaking from his natural understanding, God came and overshadowed, or enveloped Peter, James and John with His presence. Jesus is the head of the body of Christ and the other three men are part of the body. It is at this time that God

We may be able to count the seeds in an apple, but only God knows how many apples will become fruit bearing seeds from just one seed. You are that one seed!

says, *"This is my beloved Son: hear him."* God revealed the resurrection life of the body of Christ before Calvary. He demonstrated to the disciples that they were the body of Christ. They were only to live their life in the flesh with the mind of Jesus Christ, not the understanding of natural man. What took place was so far out from their comprehension that they could not tell anyone at that time. The things of God are foolish to our natural understanding. God is telling the disciples to hear His son, not just the voice of Jesus, but also the witness of His voice that is already resident within us.

When we are in the Light as He is the Light, the word is SONSHIP. Jesus is the first fruit of many. When Jesus became sin, His soul needed these men to connect with what He was experiencing in Gethsemane. Back in Genesis, when Adam named (gave nature or character) to all the animal kingdom, it came through his soul. His soul was removed from his side and became woman. After he ate of the Tree of Knowledge of Good and Evil, Adam named the woman Eve meaning the mother of all living. Her character has been passed to all humankind through the ages.

In Mark 14: 36 Jesus says, *"My soul is exceeding sorrowful unto* (into) *death: tarry ye here, and watch."* This is unique for Jesus to use the word death. He always used the word sleep to refer to death, but in this instance, he means a literal understanding of death. Jesus purposefully uses two different languages when He goes to pray. He addresses God as "Abba" meaning daddy, a term of endearment; and He says, "Father" identifying His genealogy or family. Keep in mind that at this moment He had become sin. Jesus knew that there would be a day that people would remember the language of character and genealogy, and the language of identity in the spirit.

In verse 36 Jesus is talking with the voice of the first Adam as He goes into death, *"all things are possible unto thee; take away this cup* (will of fallen

Much of the body of Christ in the earth are like dead men walking. They may have a ticket to heaven when they die, but they are no earthly good for the Kingdom of God in their flesh.

men) *from me; nevertheless not what I will, but what thou wilt."* Jesus was praying the prayer that the first Adam should have prayed back in Genesis instead of trying to justify and hide himself before God.

While Jesus is dying, the three men that went with Him to the mount of transfiguration and saw heaven open are now sleeping. Jesus did not rebuke them once, but three times: sleeping while death is transforming the outer, middle, and inner courts of the temple of God. Jesus was not mad at the men, but had to say those words to the earth to testify what humanity had been doing. They were alive in the flesh, but asleep in the spirit.

Ephesians 1:4-6

"According as he hath chosen us in him before the foundation of the world, that we should be holy and without blame before him in love: Having predestinated us unto the adoption of children by Jesus Christ to himself, according to the good pleasure of his will, To the praise of the glory of his grace, wherein he hath made us accepted in the beloved."

John 15:27

"And ye also shall bear witness, because ye have been with me from the beginning."

Job 38:1-7

"Then the LORD answered Job out of the whirlwind, and said, Who is this that darkeneth counsel by words without knowledge? Gird up now thy loins like a man; for I will demand of thee, and answer thou me. Where wast thou when I laid the foundations of the earth? declare, if thou hast understanding. Who hath laid the measures thereof, if thou knowest? Or

who hath stretched the line upon it? Whereupon are the foundations thereof fastened? Or who laid the corner stone thereof; when the morning stars sang together, and all the sons of God shouted for joy?"

God is telling Job to wake up and remember who he was before the foundations of the world. The morning stars are singing because the sons of God, or the Lights of the world, are in the earth.

John 17:5-24

"And now, O Father, glorify thou me **with thine own self (when I am you)** *with the glory* **which I had with thee before the world was (before Genesis 1:1)**. *I have manifested thy name unto the men which thou gave me out* (before) *of the world: thine they were* (they belonged to God before the world was created), *and thou gave them me; and they have kept thy word* (we were with Him in the beginning). *Now they have known that all things whatsoever thou hast given me are of thee. For I have given unto them the words which thou gave me; and they have received them, and have known surely that I came out from thee, and they have believed that thou didst send me* (we knew all about what Jesus did in the beginning. We just needed our Lights to be "turned on" by the Holy Spirit to wake us up). *I pray for them: I pray not for the world, but for them which thou hast given me; for they are thine. And* **all mine are thine and thine are mine; and I am glorified in them.** *And now I am no more in the world, but these are in the world, and I come to thee. Holy Father, keep through thine own name those whom thou hast given me that* **they may be one, as we are.** *While I was with them in the world, I kept them in thy name: those that thou gave me I have kept, and none of them is lost, but the son of perdition; that the scripture might be fulfilled. And now come I to thee; and these things I speak in the world, that they might have my joy fulfilled in themselves. I have given them thy word; and the world hath hated them, because they are not of the world, even as I am not of the world.* **I pray not that thou should take them out of the world,** *but that thou should keep them from the evil.* **They are not of the world, even as I**

am not of the world. *Sanctify them through thy truth: thy word is truth. As thou hast sent me into the world, even so have I also sent them into the world. And for their sakes I sanctify myself, that they also might be sanctified through the truth. Neither pray I for these alone, but for them also which shall believe on me through their word;* **That they all may be one; as thou, Father, art in me, and I in thee, that they also may be one in us: that the world may believe that thou hast sent me. And the glory which thou gave me I have given them; that they may be one, even as we are one: I in them, and thou in me, that they may be made perfect in one;** *and that the world may know that thou hast sent me, and hast loved them, as thou hast loved me.* **Father, I will** (will of Jesus) *that they also, whom thou hast given me,* **be with me where I am; that they may behold my glory,** *which thou hast given me: for thou loved me* **before** *the foundation of the world."*

Jesus is praying a prayer of confirmation that the work is finished. He gave us the power to connect our eternal identity with time. Jacob prophesied this in Genesis 28 as a ladder or staircase with those that are heavenly minded would be able to be in this world, but not of this world.

Genesis 28:11-19

"And he lighted upon a certain place, and tarried there all night, because the sun was set; and he took of the stones of that place, and put them for his pillows, and lay down in that place to sleep. And he dreamed, and behold a ladder set up on the earth, and the top of it reached to heaven: and behold the angels of God ascending and descending on it. And, behold, the LORD stood above it, and said, I am the LORD God of Abraham thy father, and the God of Isaac: the land whereon thou lies, to thee will I give it, and to thy seed; And thy seed shall be as the dust of the earth, and thou shall spread abroad to the west, and to the east, and to the north, and to the south: and in thee and in thy seed shall all the families of the earth be blessed. And, behold, I am with thee, and will keep thee in all places whither thou goes, and will bring thee again into this land; for I will not leave thee, until I have done

that which I have spoken to thee of. And Jacob awaked (understanding of God) *out of his sleep* (ignorance), *and he said, surely the LORD is in this place; and I knew it not. And he was afraid, and said, how dreadful this place is! This is none other but the house of God, and this is the gate of heaven. And Jacob rose up early in the morning, and took the stone* (the word of God) *that he had put for his pillows* (the mind of Christ), *and set it up for a pillar* (foundation of understanding the things of God), *and poured oil upon the top of it* (Holy Spirit anointed the revelation). *And he called the name of that place Bethel* (where God is within us)*: but the name of that city was called Luz* (old Adam nature) *at the first.*"

Hebrews 2:10

"*For it became him, for whom are **all things**, and by whom are **all things**, in bringing many sons* (of God) *unto glory* (shining as Light with their identity of the Father), *to make the captain of their salvation* (Jesus is the head of the body) *perfect through sufferings.*"

1 Peter 1:8

"*Whom having not seen, ye love; in whom, though now ye see him not, yet believing, ye rejoice with joy unspeakable and full of glory.*" This is God's definition of you today. Today we are full of glory or Light as He is Light. Some of us may not have had the switched turned on yet, but we all will in His timing.

Psalms 17:15

"*As for me, I will behold thy face* (His identity is my identity) *in righteousness: I shall be satisfied, when I awake* (receive revelation knowledge from the Holy Spirit), *with thy likeness* (I was created in His image and likeness)."

Psalms 57:7-11

"My heart is fixed, O God, my heart is fixed: I will sing and give praise. Awake up, my glory; awake, psaltery and harp: I myself will awake early. I will praise thee, O Lord, among the people: I will sing unto thee among the nations. For thy mercy is great unto the heavens, and thy truth unto the clouds. Be thou exalted, O God, above the heavens: let thy glory be above all the earth."

What are the sons of God supposed to be declaring? The greatness of the mercy of God that endures forever; and His unconditional love for all humanity whom He declares as His children. The uniqueness that Jesus demonstrated for us to follow is to believe it was finished; whether we saw it manifested or not did not matter to what we believed. Seeing what we believed in manifested should not make us a believer, but the result of us already walking by faith in believing that if God said it, it was finished. Signs and wonders were to **follow** the sons of God for those that did not believe.

Isaiah 26:19

"Thy dead men (old Adam) *shall live; together with my dead body* (of Christ) *shall they arise. Awake and sing* (come into revelation knowledge and let your true identity shine), *ye that dwell in dust* (living in the worldly ways): *for thy dew* (water of the word is in you) *is as the dew of herbs* (gives wisdom and understanding), *and the earth* (natural man) *shall cast out the dead* (death will not exist)."*

Ephesians 1:14-2:13

"Which is the earnest of our inheritance until the redemption of the purchased possession, unto the praise of his glory. Wherefore I also, after I heard of your faith in the Lord Jesus, and love unto all the saints, Cease

*not to give thanks for you, making mention of you in my prayers; That the God of our Lord Jesus Christ, the Father of glory, may give unto you the spirit of wisdom and revelation in the knowledge of him: The eyes of your understanding being enlightened; that ye **may know what is the hope of his calling, and what the riches of the glory of his inheritance in the saints,** And what is the exceeding **greatness of his power toward us who believe,** according to the working of his mighty power, Which he wrought in **Christ, when he raised him from the dead, and set him at his own right hand in the heavenly places,** Far above all principality, and power, and might, and dominion, and **every name that is named, not only in this world, but also in that which is to come:** And hath put **all things under his feet, and gave him to be the head over all things to the church, Which is his body, the fullness of him that filleth all in all."*

Continuing in Ephesians 2:1-13

*"**And you hath he quickened** (made alive), **who were dead in trespasses and sins;** Wherein time past ye walked according to the course of this world, according to the prince of the power of the air, the spirit that now worketh in the children of disobedience: Among whom also we all had our conversation in times past in the lusts of our flesh, fulfilling the desires of the flesh and of the mind; and were by nature the children of wrath, even as others. But God, who is rich in mercy, for **his great love wherewith he loved us, Even when we were dead in sins, hath quickened** (made alive) **us together with Christ, (by grace ye are saved;) And hath raised us up together, and made us sit together in heavenly places in Christ Jesus:** That in the ages to come he might show the exceeding riches of his grace in his kindness toward us through Christ Jesus. For by grace are ye saved through faith* (His faith)*; and that not of yourselves: it is the gift of God: Not of works, lest any man should boast. For we are his workmanship, created in Christ Jesus unto good works, which God hath before ordained* (before the foundation of the world) *that we should walk in them. Wherefore remember, that ye being in time past Gentiles in the flesh, who are called uncircumcision by that which is called the Circumcision in the flesh made by hands; That at that time ye were without Christ, being aliens from the commonwealth of Israel,*

*and strangers from the covenants of promise, having no hope, and without God in the world: **But now in Christ Jesus** ye who sometimes were far off* (not believing) *are made nigh by the blood of Christ.*"

The finished work of God exists whether we believe it or not. The difference is when we awake unto righteousness we then have the power and authority to BE the word of God for others that are in ignorance of the Truth.

Ephesians 2:15-17

*"Having abolished in his flesh the enmity, even the law of commandments contained in ordinances; for to make **in himself of twain one new man,** so making peace; And that he might reconcile both unto God **in one body by the cross,** having slain the enmity thereby: And came and **preached peace to you which were afar off,** and to them that were nigh.*"

God sees today all humankind as one body that was redeemed by the blood of Jesus at the cross of Calvary. The only message that exists on this side of the cross for all people can be found in His peace. There is no condemnation for anyone.

Isaiah 51:9

"Awake, awake, put on strength, O arm (branch) *of the LORD; awake, as in the ancient days* (the former ways), *in the generations of old* (before the foundation of the world).*"

Hebrews 4:3

"For we which have believed do enter into rest, as he said, as I have sworn in my wrath, if they shall enter into my rest: although the works were finished from the foundation of the world."

It is revelation knowledge that "wakes us up" to understanding that we are children of God. As children, we are heirs of HIM. In Romans 13:10-11, *"Love worketh no ill to his neighbor: therefore love is the fulfilling of the law. And that, knowing the time, that now it is high time to awake out of sleep: for now is our salvation nearer than when we believed"* Paul is not talking about going from a non-believer to a believer, but that as believers we must wake up to total redemption of body, soul, and spirit in Christ. We first believed when we were born again, but we now need to come into our full salvation.

Revelation knowledge is more than just gaining education. It knows in the deepest and the most intimate way causing a transformation of our identity. The Light that has always been within us is "turned on" by the Holy Spirit never to be turned off. 2 John 2, *"For the truth's sake, which dwelleth in us, and shall be with us forever."*

1 John 4:4-8

*"**Ye are of God**, little children, and have overcome them: because greater is he that is in you, than he that is in the world. They are of the world: therefore speak they of the world, and the world heareth them. **We are of God:** he that knoweth God heareth us; he that is not of God heareth not us. Hereby know we the spirit of truth, and the spirit of error. Beloved, let us love one another: **for love is of God; and every one that loveth is born of God, and knoweth God**. He that loveth not knoweth not God; for **God is love.**"*

God is not a love-maker, He is love. In Him there is no darkness. This has always been our true identity that the first Adam neglected to acknowledge, but over 2000 years ago Jesus reconciled this wisdom back to all mankind.

1 Corinthians 15:33-34

"Be not deceived: evil communications corrupt good manners. Awake to righteousness, and sin not; for some have not the knowledge of God: I speak this to your shame." Stop living in ignorance and awake to your Christ identity! Get out of the sleep of death. We cannot be dead and be righteous. It is impossible to be a "sinner saved by grace."

Ephesians 5:13-14

"But all things that are reproved are made manifest by the light (our God identity)*: for whatsoever doth make manifest is light* (God) *Wherefore he saith, Awake* (come into revelation knowledge) *thou that sleepest* (carnally minded) *and arise from the dead* (body, soul, and spirit), *and Christ* (His identity in you) *shall give thee light* (spirit understanding to who you really are)."*

I close this teaching with the writing of George MacDonald titled *"Inexorably Love:"*

"Such is the mercy of God that He will hold His children in the consuming fire of His distance until they pay the uttermost farthing, until they drop the purse of selfishness with all the dross that is in it, and rush inside the center of the life-giving fire whose outer circles burn."

Notes of reflection and meditation

What were your immediate thoughts as you read this chapter?

_____

_____

_____

_____

_____

_____

What seemed confusing from what you thought?

_____

_____

_____

_____

_____

_____

What was something new that you had not heard before?

_____

_____

_____

_____

_____

_____

_____

CHAPTER 3

Coming to Know the Father
Blindfolded

Mark 5:21-26:

"And when Jesus was passed over again by ship unto the other side, much people gathered unto him: and he was nigh unto the sea. And, behold, there cometh one of the rulers of the synagogue, Jairus by name; and when he saw him, he fell at his feet, And besought him greatly, saying, My little daughter lieth at the point of death: I pray thee, come and lay thy hands on her, that she may be healed; and she shall live. And Jesus went with him; and much people followed him, and thronged him. And a certain woman, which had an issue of blood twelve years, and had suffered many things of many physicians, and had spent all that she had, and was nothing bettered, but rather grew worse."

Jairus - God enlightened; light released

Woman - speaks of the church and a nation; 2 nations and 2 covenants
OT - man walking towards God
NT - man walks with God as God because he is IN Christ.

God is not Jew or Gentile, but a corporate man.

The Physicians in the OT were the heads of the synagogues.

The church (body of Christ), must be built around faith in God, the word, and prayer.

Mark 5:27, *"When she had heard of Jesus, came in the press behind, and touched his garment."*

This woman had heard about the power of Jesus, coming storms, casting out demons. His church, the body of Christ, is a place of Life. As His body, we should be driving out sickness, disease, and even death by the WORDS spoken by the mouths of the church.

"Garment" is the covering of the New Covenant. The blood of God was in the garments she touched.

Ignorance is our enemy.

Genesis 1:31

Evening and morning are defined as one day. Every spirit that would ever exist was created into existence in the beginning. The 7th day is an eternal day. Sabbath was made for man because God is the Sabbath.

My home = His Day = Sabbath.

1 Corinthians 3:5

Paul and Apollos are servants of the Lord, instruments used according to the task the Lord gave them to do. We are a portion of the work as a whole doing each our part.

Revelation 7:14

We take our tribulation and put it into the finished work of Jesus Christ washing it with His blood and it will come out white. If we do not let Jesus wash us, then we exclude ourselves. God went to the cross for Himself. It has already been His plan to reproduce Himself.

Whenever we try to make God into a line (eschatology) instead of a circle, we limit who God is. Ezekiel's wheel gives us an illustration.

Jesus was not a substitute, but God Himself.

- Romans 6:3
- Hebrews 9:28
- Galatians 2:20
- Galatians 5:24

Mark 10:46

Blindness is in place when the pollution of the soul battles with the righteousness of the Spirit; the word in you. Jesus heals the Blind Man, not woman. Religion is the only thing that can keep you from hearing the truth of the word of God (Luke 22:54-64).

It was the High Priest of that day that blind folded Jesus. It was a woman (religion) that accused Peter who knew that Jesus was the Christ.

Religion blinded the eyes of Jesus keeping them from seeing all of the finished work of God that was right in front of the people.

Isaiah 56: 9-11

"All ye beasts of the field come to devour, yea, all ye beasts in the forest. His watchmen (religion) *are blind: they are all ignorant, they are all dumb*

dogs, they cannot bark; sleeping, lying down loving to slumber (Psalm 22). *Yea, they are greedy dogs which can never have enough, and they are shepherds that cannot understand: they all look to their own way, everyone for his gain, from his quarter."*

- We must see as God sees, not as religion sees things.
- The greatest seeing is with our spirit; the eyes of the Holy Spirit.
- We can be born again and still be blind to the finished work of Jesus Christ.
- The message of Revelation is the coming together of the individual and then the corporate workings of the church.

Isaiah 42:6-9, 16

"I the Lord have called thee in righteousness, and will hold thine hand, and will keep thee, and give thee for a covenant of the people, for a light of the Gentiles; to open the blind eyes, to bring out the prisoners from the prison, and them that sit in darkness out of the prison house. I am the Lord: that is my name: and my glory will I not give to another, neither my praise to graven images. Behold, the former things are come to pass, and new things do I declare: before they spring forth I tell you of them… And I will bring the blind by a way that they knew not; I will lead them in paths that they have not known: I will make darkness light before them, and crooked things straight. These things will I do unto them, and not forsake them."

God requires us to see what is already done in heaven, not what is in front of our natural eyes. By faith in His faith and faithfulness, not our own faith, we believe the word and the power there of bringing eternity into the NOW.

John the Baptist's message was to prepare the way for us to receive our inheritance. What is our inheritance? To BE the SONS of GOD on this earth.

Matthew 15:29-31

"And Jesus departed from thence, and came nigh unto the Sea of Galilee; and went up into a mountain, and at down there. And great multitudes came unto him, having with them those that were lame, blind, dumb, maimed, and many others, and cast them down at Jesus; feet; and he healed them: Insomuch that the multitude wondered, when they saw the dumb to speak, the maimed to be whole, the lame to walk, and the blind to see; and they glorified the God of Israel."

It is not possible for us to stay as the old Adam that tried to keep us from who we are: "I am" in word and spirit.

Galatians 3:1-3

"O foolish Galatians, who hath bewitched you, that ye should not obey the truth, before whose eyes Jesus Christ hath been evidently set forth, crucified among you? This only would I learn of you, Received ye the Spirit by the works of the law, or by the hearing of faith? Are ye so foolish? Having begun in the Spirit, are ye now made perfect by the flesh?"

The blindfolding of Jesus is a representation of humanity. Being in Christ has a responsibility for us to be the word of God as Jesus illustrated and not judge with our natural eyes as religion declares. We must accept the WORD as a finished work; a people of NOW.

Notes of reflection and meditation

What were your immediate thoughts as you read this chapter?

_____

_____

_____

_____

_____

_____

What seemed confusing from what you thought?

_____

_____

_____

_____

_____

_____

What was something new that you had not heard before?

_____

_____

_____

_____

_____

_____

CHAPTER 4

Come Out from Among Them

"In Gibeon the LORD appeared to Solomon in a dream by night: and God said, Ask what I shall give thee. And Solomon said, Thou hast shewed unto thy servant David my father great mercy, according as he walked before thee in truth, and in righteousness, and in uprightness of heart with thee; and thou hast kept for him this great kindness, that thou hast given him a son to sit on his throne, as it is this day. And now, O LORD my God, thou hast made thy servant king instead of David my father: and I am but a little child: I know not how to go out or come in. And thy servant is in the midst of thy people which thou hast chosen, a great people, that cannot be numbered nor counted for multitude. Give therefore thy servant an understanding heart to judge thy people, that I may discern between good and bad: for who is able to judge this thy so great a people? And the speech pleased the Lord, that Solomon had asked this thing" (1 Kings 3:5-10).

The greatest need of the body of Christ is for each of us to have an understanding heart towards one another. Everything created is inter-connected for God; working together for His glory both in the natural and the spiritual realms; and everything is affected by the domain that surrounds us. It may be positive or negative, but we are never at any point polarized or separated from our surroundings.

In the world of thought, there is one thought that influences all other thoughts. In the world of life, one life influences all other lives. In the world of stars, one star influences all other stars. *"And he gave some, apostles; and some, prophets; and some, evangelists; and some, pastors and teachers; For the perfecting of the saints, for the work of the ministry, for the edifying of the body of Christ: Till we all come in the unity of the faith, and of the knowledge of the Son of God, unto a perfect man, unto the measure of the stature of the fullness of Christ"* (Ephesians 4:11-13).

We may seem to have separation and division in the body of Christ, but it is only for a season of working all things for His glory and perfection. Maturity is manifested when we grow up in Christ by bringing unity to the body as one.

God tells Solomon that He will give him whatever he asked for. This was a test that God was giving him to see what his focus would be if he could have anything. Solomon caused God to react. Instead of a young king desiring riches and glory for himself, he asked for the wisdom of discernment to be the best king for a people that would praise and exalted before God. Each one of us must gain the skillful, spiritual insight to make necessary proper decisions with the humbleness to understand that our human ability is not capable of naturally discerning on the level of God. It is the gift of the Spirit.

1 John 4:1

"Beloved, believe not every spirit, but try the spirits whether they are of God: because many false prophets are gone out into the world."

2 Tim 3:15-17

"And that from a child thou hast known the holy scriptures, which are able to make thee wise unto salvation through faith which is in Christ Jesus. All scripture is given by inspiration of God, and is profitable for doctrine, for reproof, for correction, for instruction in righteousness: That the man of God may be perfect, thoroughly furnished unto all good works."

Hebrews 5:8-14

"Though he were a Son, yet learned he obedience by the things which he suffered; And being made perfect, he became the author of eternal salvation unto all them that obey him; Called of God an high priest after the order of Melchisedec. Of whom we have many things to say, and hard to be uttered, seeing ye are dull of hearing. For when for the time ye ought to be teachers, ye have need that one teach you again which be the first principles of the oracles of God; and are become such as have need of milk, and not of strong meat. For every one that useth milk is unskillful in the word of righteousness: for he is a babe. But strong meat belongeth to them that are of full age, even those who by reason of use have their senses exercised to **discern** *both good and evil."*

Matthew 5:8-9

"Blessed are the pure in heart: for they shall see God. Blessed are the peacemakers: for they shall be called the children of God."

We are fools to think that God is only doing what we can relate to and understand. When man REALLY finds God, he REALLY finds himself. Man will know who he is, what he is all about, and what his purpose and destiny for being alive at this moment and hour. All men have a quest in finding God, but many settle for the emotional satisfaction instead of the identity a relationship with God offers to each of us. A true relationship with God releases a peace that surpasses our natural understanding overflowing with unconditional love, mercy, and forgiveness for others that may not deserve this love.

The writer of Hebrews tells us that we are drinking milk as babies trying to discern good and evil. Paul tells us in 1 Corinthians 11:27-31, *"Wherefore whosoever shall eat this bread, and drink this cup of the Lord, unworthily, shall be guilty of the body and blood of the Lord. But let a man examine himself, and so let him eat of that bread, and drink of that cup. For he that eateth and drinketh unworthily, eateth and drinketh damnation to himself, not discerning the Lord's body. For this cause many are weak and sickly among you, and many sleep. **For if we would judge ourselves, we should not be judged.**"*

How often do we judge others lifting ourselves up with a "holier than thee" attitude by what we discern as good or evil from the outward man? This is no different from what the religious leaders were doing during the time of Jesus. We have been called to be ambassadors, kings, and priests as Solomon was. We are in a position of sitting on the mercy seat of God with the mind of Christ looking out over the kingdom of God with His power, His authority, and His eyes. Are we discerning the Lord's body with the Father's heart to bring unity to the body of Christ, or with the heart of a child looking out for themselves seeking their own rewards of what God can give them?

Paul tells the church in 2 Corinthians 6:11-18:

"We have spoken freely to you, Corinthians, and opened wide our hearts to you. We are not withholding our affection from you, but you are withholding yours from us (Paul is being judged). *As a fair exchange–I speak as to my children–open wide your hearts also. Do not be yoked together with unbelievers* (those that are self-centered Christians). *For what do righteousness* (purity of unconditional love) *and wickedness* (conditional love) *have in common? Or what fellowship can light* (our identity in

God) *of have with darkness* (identity in religion)? *What harmony is there between Christ and Belial* (religion)? *What does a believer* (unity of Christ as one body) *have in common with an unbeliever* (I've got my ticket to heaven attitude)? *What agreement is there between the temple of God* (body of Christ) *and idols* (we are all individuals)? *For we are the temple of the living God. As God has said: "I will live with them and walk among them, and I will be their God, and they will be my people."*

> *"Therefore come out from them*
> *and be separate,*
> *says the Lord.*
>
> *Touch no unclean thing,*
> *and I will receive you."*
> *"I will be a Father to you,*
> *and you will be my sons and daughters,*
> *says the Lord Almighty"* (NIV).

God's enemies are not the "non-believers," but those that take His word and identity as His body of believers and use it to justify, condemn, and separate His body. Beware of those that you fellowship with that are wolves in sheep's clothing (religious people). *"Behold, I send you forth as sheep in the midst of wolves: be ye therefore wise as serpents, and harmless as doves"* (Matthew 10:16).

I end this teaching with the wisdom of our Father given to us through Paul in Acts 20:29-35:

> *"For I know this, that after my departing shall grievous wolves* (religion) *enter in among you, not sparing the flock* (fellowshipping with like-minded believers). *Also of your own selves shall men arise, speaking perverse* (judgmental, condemning) *things, to draw away disciples* (identity of Christ) *after them. Therefore watch, and remember, that by the space of three years I ceased*

not to warn every one night and day with tears. And now, brethren, I commend you to God, and to the word (Himself) *of his grace* (unconditional)*, which is able to build you up, and to give you an inheritance* (identity of being a son of God) *among all them* (denominations of Christianity who separate and divide the body of Christ) *which are sanctified. I have coveted no man's silver, or gold, or apparel* (no earthly or natural understanding to do God's purpose)*. Yea, ye yourselves know, that these hands* (of God) *have ministered unto my necessities* (whatever was *needed for the mission that Paul was called to do), and to them that were with me. I have shewed you all things, how that so labouring ye ought to support the weak* (those ignorant in the ways of God with mercy and love)*, and to remember the words of the Lord Jesus, how he said,* **It is more blessed to give** (unconditional love, mercy, peace, and forgiveness) *than to receive."*

Notes of reflection and meditation

What were your immediate thoughts as you read this chapter?

_____

_____

_____

_____

_____

_____

What seemed confusing from what you thought?

_____

_____

_____

_____

_____

_____

What was something new that you had not heard before?

_____

_____

_____

_____

_____

_____

CHAPTER 5

The Law versus the Grace of God

The ministry of the Apostle Paul was different from the religion that was preached by the Jewish men who were presenting the law. There is a vast difference in Old Testament concept of Judaism and the New Testament understanding of grace. However, Paul did not do away with God's teachings and instructions found in the Old Testament.

Paul was a Rabbi taught by the best. The foundation of his writings are to bring correction to particular people for particular issues. We have Paul's responses, but we do not know the question he was addressing in his response for particular culture and customs of his time period. Eighty-five percent of his writings of correction were connected with the teachings and instructions found in the Old Testament.

The key difference of our relationship with God through Jesus Christ and the grace of God versus the people of God in the Old Testament is the methodology of coming to God as Father. The law of sin and death kept mankind from entering into His presence. This is the LAW that Jesus paid the price for sin on Calvary through the atonement of His blood once and for all. This is God's Grace. We have the ability of enjoying an eternal presence with the Father through Jesus Christ as our personal Lord and Savior.

However, while we are in our natural body, we have the ability to Be the Light of the world that I still in darkness and sin. This training to reign takes the free will choice and desire to have intimacy with the Father by abiding in His teachings and instructions. He gave His children through the Torah, Psalms, and Prophets of the Old Testament.

The word "Torah" comes from the root word "ora" meaning LIGHT. God is LIGHT. When we search the micro level of mankind's chromosomes and DNA, we find the Hebrew letters in our blood. Jesus Christ is the WORD, the Alpha and Omega, the entire Hebrew Alphabet. He became the WORD, the Torah in the flesh, and dwells among, in the midst of mankind today (John 1:14).

Paul sends a letter to the Galatians saying, *"I marvel that ye are so soon removed from him that called you into the grace of Christ unto another gospel: Which is not another; but there be some that trouble you, and would pervert the gospel of Christ. But though we, or an angel from heaven, preach any other gospel unto you than that which we have preached unto you, let him be accursed."* (Gal. 1:5-6) KJV

The Galatians were turning to Judaism, which was being taught by the converted Christians, after Paul had presented grace. Jewish Christians were telling them that they needed law along with grace to enter into the Kingdom of God. They were perverting the gospel of Christ. The gospel of Christ is a gospel of Grace. It is a gospel where God first comes to you; as

For God so loved, He gave love (Himself) while we were still in darkness and sin. God's love in us must be given away. This is a basic principle of His identity and character.

you fellowship and receive God you find out that He is in you; then as you realize that He is in you, the revelation of His identity and nature will be manifested out of you. This is the gospel of Christ.

There is no place in this message of grace for man to do anything. It is an unveiling and a revealing the heart of Father God that has been placed in each of us when man was created in His image. The Father loves each of us with an unconditional love. He provided a way of life into His presence that is not by a performance or code of ethics. Christ in us has already fulfilled all the righteous requirements of the law setting us free from the bondage of the law.

The gospel of Grace does not say that we can live any way we want to, but that as the veil is pulled back and grace is manifested; our desires are transformed into His calling on our lives. There is nothing lawless about the gospel of Grace, yet at the same time, we cannot think that there are certain things or ways that we must act or feel in order to come into His presence. The gospel of Christ forms the very nature and heart of God within our conscious. It becomes manifested by faith in God and His faithfulness. Not by our works to try to have enough faith.

Grace is God's life in us, being formed in us, and coming to maturity in us so that when others see us, they see the Father of all. Grace is a divine enabler with no requirements to our flesh. We were crucified with him, and today we live by faith in the grace of Christ.

Grace produces God's seed of unconditional love, His life, His nature in you.

The word "law" given to us through the translators from Hebrew to Greek as the word "nomos" removed the hidden treasures of LIFE the Father gave us in the Torah.

The law of sin and death produces the carnal nature of good and evil. The law was given to carnal men to restrain the natural man's flesh.

Grace replaces the law of sin and death, but not the teaching and instructions of the Father that are still applicable in what we sow we reap on the earth. Grace is the Melchizedek priesthood bringing to us the bread of His word and the wine of His enjoyment. As we are able to receive grace, it must be given away. That is all part of our God identity of unconditional love. The process of giving will cause trials and tribulations within us and around us where the law will try to intervene and take control.

Grace brings gifts to us without making demands on us. God knows what gifts He has bestowed on each of us, and how He wants those gifts to be manifested. It is not up to us to force ourselves to be a certain way as a Christian because of what religion says. When we receive the peace of who we are in Christ we will respond to our identity we have in Him. Unconditional love draws us to the Father with a desire to have a closer relationship to Him.

The law of sin and death produces good and evil out of our carnal nature. It causes us to choose good or evil. If we choose well we expect a blessing. If we choose evil then our conscious will challenge us. The law never stops putting demands on us to where we will never feel good enough or holy enough. We will always feel we need to try to be a better person by striving to do things right according to what the church believes.

Grace says that you are already a spiritual being with the same nature and character as your heavenly Father. Grace produces a dependence on God for everything. The law tries to justify a "buddy" system with God. In our being is the fullness of all that God is. Everything that we need will come to us because the essence of who He is already is within us.

Jesus removed the law of sin and death, but not the teaching and instructions of the Father given to Moses. Without these, we don't know how to prepare ourselves as a bride for the return of Jesus Christ on the earth.

The law of sin and death produces a self-dependence. You must do it. You must make a choice to be saved; to be a better person; to go to heaven. Grace says you already have it all. In His timing according to the wholeness of His creation, the Holy Spirit will remove the veil of our spiritual understanding that has been blinded by our carnal mind.

When Christians judge others for not keeping the dos and don'ts that have been established in the church they create a modern day Pharisee among themselves. They think because they were able to live a certain life of self-control that everyone else should be able to also. When others are not able to, they are looked down upon as not being good enough for the Kingdom of God.

Grace produces a dependence on God for everything. We do not need a good self-image of our natural man, but a good understanding of our God identity that is within us. Once the essence of His life begins to flow in us, we cannot be anything but the manifestation of whom He has created.

The law of sin and death produces a selfish/self-centered love. "I will love you if you love me." "I love you because you are good to me." However, the very moment you do something against me, my love becomes critical towards you. God's love enables us to love those that are not easy to love without expecting love in return.

Grace produces a godly image...law produces a good self-image.

The more we experience His love, the more His love will flow from our being to others. Being in the Kingdom of God allows us to love without a selfish motive. We already have all that we need when we know that we are today in the presence of God. A Melchizadek priest does not require love from anyone, but can give love unconditionally. They have everything they need, the source of all life flowing through them.

The law can only produce sin and death stirring up the carnal man to be something that he is not. Grace reveals to us that His law is in us; we are saved by His life that arises in us. There is no salvation in the mind of the carnal man. It is within our spirit that must come forth crucifying our mind that tries to control with legal understanding.

Grace produces the fruit of the Spirit; love, joy, peace, longsuffering, gentleness, goodness, faith, meekness, and temperance (Gal. 5:22-23). With these fruits, there is no law. Grace allows us to live a life that is totally controlled by the Holy Spirit. To be filled with the Spirit is to be controlled and moved by Him, Jesus Christ. The law controls us by religious spirits.

One of the big issues that Martin Luther had with the Catholic Church was the selling of indulgence to buy people out of purgatory. If you paid the priest, you could buy time for your relatives to be out of hell. Today, we do not call it selling of indulgence, but many ministries are practicing the same concept. They approach the body of Christ by stirring their emotions to obtain financial involvement. Many times people feel guilty if they do not send money for something. Then if something happens to them personally, they believe it is because they did not give to a ministry.

Christian telethons call it sowing into seed faith offering. When we believe that it takes a certain pastor to pray for us to receive a blessing because that person has a greater anointing, then we are being trapped into a legalist realm of good and evil instead of grace.

All of us are one with the same anointing from the same Holy

> *Jesus told us that the Almighty Creator was His Father and God, then He said that God was the Almighty to each of us, but that He was also our Father. Some people may have developed a closer relationship with the Father, but we all have equal opportunity to be as intimate with Him as we desire.*

Spirit. Grace produces one new man on this earth. There is nothing we can do to **bring** the Kingdom of God. Jesus finished it all at Calvary over 2000 years ago. Our responsibility is to share the good news that the Kingdom of God is here now within you.

A corporate man is coming forth in the body of Christ as one new man. We live by God from the enjoyment of God that came through Jesus Christ. The law came through Moses, but grace (enjoyment) came through Jesus. As the one new man is growing in consciousness on this earth, we realize we have the same Father and the same life. We condemn no man, and only judge with a righteous judgment desiring to release all of creation from the bondage of corruption. This is happening today being manifested in every man according to God's timing in each of our lives.

Grace produces the one new man growing and coming to maturity in our earthly bodies. It does not matter that we may be Baptist, Lutheran, Catholic, etc. We can analyze our differences and see that those things really do not matter in the eyes of God. That what is important is that we come together in the unity of faith in Jesus Christ who is Lord over all.

The law of sin and death produces division in the body of Christ. It creates all the different denominations and doctrines that separate and divide God's people.
They believe that serving God is doing things right according to their interpretation and understanding of scripture.

If we will focus on the oneness of divine grace living as Jesus lived, we will see the manifestation of the sons of God on this earth. Jesus is the vine and we are the branch. He is our source of all. Law is the creator of all division, but grace is the life that produces fruit as the Holy Spirit flows from the vine to the branches.

It is Christ in YOU, the hope of glory (Colossians 1:27). The only things that will bring recognition are the oneness in us with the Father. The substance of who others are is the same as what we are. Each of us has Christ within us, the essence of the Father; His DNA. The first Adam had it, but denied its existence. The last Adam, Jesus Christ, restored by reconciliation our identity in HIM. *"Ye are of God, little children…God is love…as he is, so are we in this world"* (I John 4: 4a, 16b, 17b).

When we understand that our true nature and the nature of others is Spirit, we cannot steal from them, do harm against them, or hurt them in any way. To do so would be to do it against God our Father. The godly decision you make for yourself will not only be the best for you, but for your family, friends, and those that come across your path each day. A godly decision that is best for you is one that is based on grace and unconditional love from the Father. When we live in this realm for ourselves, then those around us will receive grace and unconditional love from us.

Grace represents Christ…Law represents the old, carnal man. Law produces mystery Babylon. Grace produces the New Jerusalem…the city of God that is among us now. (Notes taken from Gary Sigler's teaching "Christ vs. Religion," Sigler Ministries, PO Box 26695, Winston Salem, NC 27114-6695.)

Notes of reflection and meditation

What were your immediate thoughts as you read this chapter?

_____
_____
_____
_____
_____
_____

What seemed confusing from what you thought?

_____
_____
_____
_____
_____
_____

What was something new that you had not heard before?

_____
_____
_____
_____
_____
_____

CHAPTER 6

The Law of Faith

Hebrews 11

For us to be able to begin this study, we must first be willing to go beyond the position of memorizing Scripture. We need to be at the place that we can apprehend the Spirit of the Word where we become convicted by the Word we are hearing. For those that have walked with the Lord for a long time it is easy to become numb by the memory of what we have gleaned from the Word in the past, and not be sensitive to what it is saying to us today. When we hear a familiar Scripture, our challenge is to receive it as if we had never heard it before, instead of falling into the repetition of repeating the Scripture from familiarity without really paying attention to what it is saying.

Hebrews 11:1-3

"Now faith is the substance of things hoped for, the evidence of things not seen. For by it the elders obtained a good report. **Through faith we understand that the worlds were framed by the word of God, so that things which are seen were not made of things which do appear."**

Read carefully what the Spirit of God says: what is seen, or what we see in the natural, does not owe its existence to what is visible. Everything is created by the unseen, or by Spirit; this creative, unrestricted power, from which ALL things come into being. According to Hebrews 11:3, it is through faith that we understand the worlds (plural) were framed by the WORD of God. Anything invisible is meaningless unless it has a form. Has anyone ever seen a demon or a devil? What we have seen is something that is in opposition to God, and we have given the invisible thing credit by calling it a demon, yet it is meaningless without a form. In Ephesians 4:17 we are instructed, *"Neither give place to the devil."* For something to be real, a thing can only be known by its manifested form. It does not mean that it does not exist, but that it is meaningless without form.

Our thoughts have the potential to become reality. Be careful of what Armageddon may be developing between your ears.

Example: What is electricity? No one would know unless it was manifested through one of its forms such as light, heat, or power, yet it has always been in existence, even before it was discovered. If we were to try to consider electricity without its manifestation, we would be creating an unknown with our imagination, yet never really knowing the real form.

We read in Isaiah 43:10, *"Ye are my witnesses, saith the LORD, and my servant whom I have chosen: that ye may know and believe me, and understand that I am he:* **before me there was no God formed, neither shall there be after me.***"*

Even God, being Spirit, without being visible, remains meaningless without form. Without Him coming into manifestation, we end up relying upon our imaginations to define God. Again, anything invisible is meaningless if we do not see its manifested form. Reality can only be known by what we experience of its tangible form (electricity is known by its manifested form as; light, power, heat, etc.).

God, who is the ultimate one person in the universe, would have remain meaningless to us; however, He does have and has had from eternity a manifested form of Himself called the Word, Jesus Christ, to manifest His person. Malachi 2:10 says, *"Have we not all one father? Hath not one God created us?"*

According to John 1:1-2, Jesus Christ was called the "Word" who was in the beginning with God and who was God: *"In the beginning was the Word, and the Word was with God, and the Word was God. The same was in the beginning with God."* **A 'word' is a fixed, final form of a thought.** Jesus Christ had from eternity manifested God in form by being called the WORD; His Son. God saw in thought, spoke the thought, and manifested a form of the thought. It is by the 'word' that the thought moves into action.

Let us look at Genesis 1:1-3: *"In the beginning God created* (thought) *the heaven and the earth. And the earth was without form, and void; and darkness was upon the face of the deep.* (There is no word spoken yet to give form to the thought.) *And the Spirit of God moved upon the face of the waters. And God said* (thought becomes manifested), *Let there be light: and there was light* (let there be ME)."

The "I AM that I am" spoken of in Exodus 3 by God can be processed as "I Am that I BE." The word Torah comes from Hebrew root word "ora" which means "Light". As God is Light (1 John 1:5), we too have His Light within us through Jesus Christ. Jesus said, *""You are the light of the world. A town built on a hill cannot be hidden."* (Matthew 5:14).

The Son becomes HIMSELF (GOD), the WORD in action, which explains what Paul meant in Colossians when saying that by HIM all things are created; *"Giving thanks unto the Father, which hath made us meet to be partakers of the inheritance of the saints in light* (Himself, the Word)*: Who hath delivered us from the power of darkness* (ignorance of our own understanding), *and hath translated* (already changed) *us into the kingdom of his dear Son: In whom we have* (within us now) *redemption through his blood, even the forgiveness of sins: Who is the image* (manifested form) *of the invisible God, the firstborn* (seed identity) *of every creature* (mankind)*: For by him were **all** things created* (all thoughts), *that are in heaven, and that are in earth, visible and invisible, whether they be thrones, or dominions, or principalities, or powers: all things were created by him, and for him: And he is before **all** things, and by him **all** things consist"* (Col. 1:12-17).

Going back to John 1:3, *"**All** things were made by **him**; and without **him** was not anything made that was made."* The Son becomes HIMSELF, the WORD in action, and by HIM, all things were created. In the beginning was the WORD and all things were made by HIM. This is not saying that God did something to make something. This is not magic where God created something out of Himself that became something else. All things came out of HIM.

The WORD was with God in the beginning. GOD who is invisible created WORD in the mind of GOD. The WORD was spoken by HIMSELF in the beginning to bring form to the thought. The thought moved into action to become the WORD (the SON), and the law of sowing and reaping was created: The thought, the word, the deed: Father, Son, and Holy Spirit. The eternal God, as a living person, speaks His WORD of self-manifestation into visibility. The Begotten Son, the WORD, becomes flesh. The Son himself becomes the WORD in action, and HE creates all things, out of HIM.

God did this when He said, "let there **BE** light; or become light." The law of creation is Father, Son, and Holy Ghost. It is more than a Biblical triune manifestation of God; it is also more than what some religions consider as three gods. The Lord our God is ONE. He is ALL Spirit and an All-knowing mind. This Spirit is the WORD, which was with God, and who was God, and the WORD became the manifestation (the fixed form of the thought) of God as flesh. All things were created by HIM and out of HIM by the law of creation.

God spoke the word "BE" and He was manifested in completion. There was no striving, hope, or effort to obtain something. When God spoke, it was finished. No word was spoken to "see" if something would be manifested. No efforts were made in "hope." The WORD was spoken with the authority of His BEING and the conviction of KNOWING the purpose of His Father that caused the (origin of the thought) WORD to become a manifested form.

The SON (the WORD) made a declaration of what we all now call FAITH, yet He declared it as a command. It was **not** something He desired as a hope, but He spoke it with the conviction of BEING so that the command of God to become LIGHT became LIGHT, and there was LIGHT, all in one moment. Time had no place. The conviction of BEING demands more than just a verbal word, but a command of Spirit: BE it.

The Law of Faith manifests all creation: Father, Son, and Holy Ghost. When we understand this principle, we can then look at Hebrews Chapter 11 to see how faith operated from the very beginning of the Bible. According to the Law of Faith: The beginning **is** God. With the mind of God, there is the formation of thought and the conviction of the purpose of **knowing**; by the command and conviction of purpose the Spirit **spoke**; what was spoken had to be **manifested**. This is the pattern God set in the beginning for those who come after HIM.

Genesis 1:1-4

"In the beginning God (He is the beginning) *created the heaven and the earth. And the earth was without form, and void; and darkness was upon the face of the deep. And the Spirit of God **moved** upon the face of the*

*waters. And God **said**, Let there be light: and there was light. And God **saw** the light, that it was good:"*

It is necessary for us to first have a vision of His will in order to give the Spirit something to move on. There needs to be a conviction of faith, in order for us to see the manifestation of what has already been seen in thought. We must be willing to remove any limits within our own creative ability so that we do not hinder what God is doing by His power and authority within us. Paul tells us in Ephesians 3:20, *"Now unto him that is able to do exceeding abundantly above all that we ask or think, according to the power that worketh in us."* If we have any preconceived anticipations of personal desires that do not line up with the WORD, we will hinder what God is doing. There must be an elevation beyond the activity of our own creative thought for the release of the first principle of faith: An inward seeing with the mind of Christ and having the conviction of faith in KNOWING the outcome of the WORD because we understand what it means to be sons of God. This faith is not a working of something we can do, but simply trusting in the faith or faithfulness of the Creator to his creation.

> *God enjoys speaking to us while we are asleep in dreams and visions to share with us how to spend our daylight time. Our soul tends to be quieter when we sleep so our spirit can listen to the Father.*

The **Law of Creation** demands that the pattern be Father, Son, and Holy Ghost:

* ★ "Beginning" - Father: God saw in thought (**moved upon the face**)
* ★ "God (Elohim)" - Son (Christ): God said (**WORD spoke**)
* ★ "Spirit" - Holy Ghost: (God saw - **manifestation of thought**)

In His conviction of BEING, the Son/Word makes a declaration of faith, which is also the command to become light. The conviction of BEING declares, not just as a verbal command, but also as a command of Spirit, "Be it done" so it is; "Let there be," and so it is. This is how faith has worked from the very beginning of Scripture:

The Spirit "Father" moved on what He is **going to see**. Nothing happens until the Father moves. God did not move because He saw it. The Law of Creation with God is first, it is finished and then it is created in thought. Man creates by what he sees first (visible) in the natural (logic, reason, knowledge) and then the spiritual, but God moves by what He sees in the invisible first. For us to see Christ, God first had to bring us Adam. Man's understanding requires there to be a "first" in order for there to be a "last."

God creates from the invisible (what is "last" to man) and brings it into the visible (what is "first" to man). Man starts something to finish it, but God starts because it is finished first. The Book of Revelation is the "end" in man's way of understanding; but for God, it is the beginning, which came before Genesis. God starts something to finish it; but the truth is, He has already finished everything first and is manifesting it last. God MOVES (Father) on what He is going to SEE; then God SAYS (Son); then God SEES (Holy Spirit) what He moved on. Nothing happens until God moves.

Father God created everything in His beginning, "*to make all men see what is the fellowship of the mystery, which from the beginning of the world hath been hid **in God**, who created **all things** by Jesus Christ* (WORD)*"* (Ephesians 3:9).

The earth (humankind) was without form, void, empty, dark, without understanding, and completely ignorant. The Spirit of God (Father) moved. The conviction of that move declares, or speaks a command of Spirit (Son). What He said is manifested (Holy Ghost). Faith is the substance and the evidence. **Nothing happens until the Spirit**

of God in us moves. Then, as a son of God, we speak, and the Holy Ghost manifests what the Spirit of God in us saw.

Colossians 1:15-19:

"Who is the image of the invisible God, the firstborn of every creature: For by him (in him) *were all things created, that are in heaven, and that are in earth, visible and invisible, whether they be thrones* (lordships), *or dominions, or principalities* (sovereignties or authorities), *or powers: all things were created by him* (through him), *and for him: And he is before all things, and by him all things consist* (have cohesion in him). *And he is the head of the body, the church: who is the beginning* (ecclesia, sovereign), *the firstborn from the dead* (earth); *that in all things he might have the preeminence. For it pleased the Father that in him should all fullness dwell."*

He created Heaven and earth. In Him is ALL created. There is nothing that is created which did not come into being except by Him or out of Him. In Him is all created: Heaven and earth; authorities and powers; thrones or lordships and sovereignties. All is created IN HIM, THROUGH HIM, BY HIM, and FOR HIM. He is before ALL, and ALL have their cohesion in Him who is the head of ALL creation. Firstborn…sovereign.

The Spirit way is the Faith way (Hebrews 11). We cannot please God except by the Law of Faith: God sees (invisible form); God speaks; God manifests what He sees (visible form). The Son of God is ALL creation; the beginning of all creation. Nothing exists except through Him. This is a law. This is not about a man named Jesus, but about God the Son (Elohim) THE CHRIST (in the beginning, God). Created in HIM are all things and by Him all things consist. This sovereignty is the firstborn of many brethren (Romans 8:29). God shows us that IN HIM are all created.

Again, let us read Colossians 1:15-17:

*"Who is the image of the invisible God, the firstborn of every creature: For by him were **all things created, that are in heaven, and that are in earth, visible and invisible, whether they be thrones, or dominions, or principalities, or powers: all things were created by him, and for him:** And he is before all things, and by him all things consist."*

Everything that exists has its cohesion in Him and through Him. Ponder a moment, and let this thought really sink into your understanding. Jesus Christ is the head, the ecclesia of the body who is THE Sovereign; THE firstborn. Second born is just as sovereign; third born is just as sovereign, etc. The law of God is from the Father (what He saw in the invisible) to the Son (the WORD spoken); to the Spirit (manifestation of what was seen by the Father). Life moved from the Spirit (law of faith) to the spirit. Likewise, He who is Spirit moves upon our spirit, and by His conviction of faith we see the invisible and speak the word because we know the Father has already finished all things.

The SON and the sons have an inner substance of the same Holy Spirit. Out of them, everything is created that is created. The reality is that there is nothing outside of us. This is why Jesus said in Mark 11:22-23, *"And Jesus answering saith unto them, **Have faith in God**** (your identity in Him). *For verily I say unto you, That whosoever shall say unto this mountain* (oppositions of life), *Be thou removed, and be thou cast into the sea* (humanity); *and shall not doubt in his heart* (for out of the heart the mouth speaks), *but shall believe that those things which he saith shall* (already finished) *come to pass; he shall have whatsoever he saith."* This is not believing because you see it first manifested, but believing it is already completed in Him and confessing this belief with your mouth.

Mark 11:24-25:

"Therefore I say unto you, what things so ever ye desire, when ye pray (there must be communion with God as your Heavenly Father), *believe that ye receive them, and ye shall have them. And when ye stand praying, forgive, if ye have ought against any: that your Father also which is in heaven may forgive you your trespasses."*

Notice that in order to come into communion with God we must first forgive those who have caused conflict in our life. It does not matter what the reason might be. If our thoughts are focused on anything other than God, we cannot come into His presence. Jesus takes this connection of forgiveness and faith a step further in Matthew 5:21-26:

"You have heard that it was said to those of old, 'You shall not murder,' and whoever murders will be in danger of the judgment. But I say to you that whoever is angry with his brother without a cause shall be in danger of the judgment. And whoever says to his brother, 'Raca!' shall be in danger of the council. But whoever says, 'You fool!'

Agreeing with your adversary quickly will empty the gun sooner, and allow God to step in faster with His solutions.

*shall be in danger of hell fire. Therefore if you bring your gift to the altar, and there remember that **your brother has something against you**, leave your gift there before the altar, and go your way. First be reconciled to your brother, and then come and offer your gift. **Agree with your adversary quickly**, while you are on the way with him, lest your adversary deliver you to the judge, the judge hand you over to the officer, and you are thrown into prison. Assuredly, I say to you, you will by no means get out of there till you have paid the last penny"* (NKJV).

Notice in Matthew that Jesus considers the action of committing murder to be the same as speaking angry words towards another. He also emphasizes that when we come before God in prayer, we may have an untroubled heart, but if someone else has something against us, we are to resolve the issue by agreeing with him or her; not by trying to justify ourselves. We are to ask them for forgiveness and allow the peace of God in us to rectify our oneness in Christ despite the justification our natural understanding may try to bring up.

The Spirit way is the Faith way. He who is Spirit moves upon our spirit allowing the conviction of who we are in Christ to be manifested. It is from this position that mountains, or oppositions, in our life are removed. This intimate knowing of Spirit with spirit is obstructed when the peace, which surpasses all understanding, is missing. The grace of God is sufficient, but it does not allow for the manifestation of miracles. As children, we learn that grace is sufficient, but when one knows who he is in Christ, it is not miracles or signs and wonders that are sought after, but the manifestation of sonship in the earth.

The Law of Faith becomes active in our lives when the Holy Spirit has moved upon our spirits, and we are able to declare what we know because we have seen what the Father has seen. The sons of God have this inner substance of connection to the Holy Spirit because they are in Christ and Christ is in them, but they are often hindered because of "spirit attitude" which is the preparation for "spirit action." We must remember that nothing owes its existence to what is visible, but to what is invisible created in the beginning in God. Faith cannot function until our spirits have first experienced an inward response of intercourse (marriage covenant) with the Holy Spirit. This is a Holy of Holies experience where we are seated with Him in heavenly places in the now. The "Logos" or WORD speaks the "rhema" word to our spirits, creating His power and authority in us, so that we can speak with the creative power of the Father.

Paul tells us in Ephesians 1:3-4, *"Blessed be the God and Father of our Lord Jesus Christ, who hath* (already completed) *blessed us with all* (everything) *spiritual blessings in heavenly places in Christ: According* (saw by the Father in the beginning) *as he hath* (completed by what He saw in the Son) *chosen us in him before the foundation of the world* (manifestation of the natural), *that we should* (we are already, holy because God does not make a mistake) *be holy and without blame before him in love* (unconditional)."

Ephesians 1:20-23

"*Which he wrought in Christ, when He raised Him from the dead, and set Him at His own right hand in the heavenly places, far above all principality, and power, and might, and dominion, and every name* (every word that has been created) *that is named, not only in this world, but also in that which is to come* (paste, present, and future): *And hath* (already completed everything) *put ALL things under His feet* (the church), *and gave Him to be the head over ALL things to the church, which is His body, the FULLNESS of Him that filleth ALL in ALL.*"

Ephesians 2:4-6

"*But God, who is rich in mercy, for his great love* (unconditional) *wherewith he loved us, even when we were dead in sins, hath* (He has already raised us up from the dead) *quickened us together* (He has already given mankind His Life as one body) *with Christ, (by grace ye are saved;) And hath* (finished) *raised us* (we are already in Christ) *up together, and made us* (spirit beings) *sit together* (rest in our knowing that we are His children now) *in heavenly places* (Holy of Holies, we are spirit beings) *in Christ Jesus:*"

Ephesians 3:10-12

"*To the intent that **now** unto the principalities and powers in heavenly places might be known by the church the manifold wisdom of God, according* *to the eternal purpose which he purposed in Christ Jesus our Lord: In whom we have boldness and access with confidence by the faith of Him."*

To move the mountains or obstacles in our life we must apply the Law of Faith: Father, Son, and Holy Ghost. Our minds (believing/ understanding) will also be seated with Him in heavenly places, when we know who we are in Christ. We cannot be in that posture unless we have first forgiven those who have trespassed against us, and have asked for forgiveness from those that we have offended. There must be absolutely no cause for our adversary to find any judgment against us in order for us to be seated with Christ in the Holy of Holies or mercy seat of God.

Again, when the Holy Spirit inwardly moves upon our spirits, creating a conviction of Faith, we will be able to declare the Truth we know, and we will see in manifestation what we have seen in spirit reality.

Again, the **Law of Creation** demands that the pattern be Father, Son, and Holy Ghost:

★ "Beginning" - Father; God saw in thought (**moved upon the face/identity**)
★ "God (Elohim)" - Son (Christ); God said (**WORD spoke**)
★ "Spirit" - Holy Ghost; (God saw - **manifestation of thought**)

For this reason, it is impossible to please God, or even to see and understand what He is doing, outside of the parameters of His Law of Creation and Faith.

"Spirit attitude" depends on soul power as the engine that activates our spirits. If our souls are depending upon the manifestation of what is seen versus what is said by faith, there will be a hindrance to understanding what God is doing. We will not be as sensitive to the move of the Spirit because our souls will be trying to justify and analyze the situation with our carnal understanding. Most Christians pray with the desire to see God move. This puts them in a position of justifying what went wrong when the move does not happen the way they thought it should. This in turn ignites the emotions and senses to where the soul causes a move that is not of God, but because they are Christians, they believe it is God, not realizing that it was really their own soulish words that caused the manifestation.

When there is a move of Spirit, it can only come by "spirit action" which is dependent upon "spirit attitude" being in perfect unity with God. In the Holy of Holies God can only commune with His own identity, nothing of soul life can enter into the throne room of God.

We must understand that the "attitude of spirit" is the posture and alignment we have as preparation for "spirit action" in causing the sovereignty of God to move in our lives. It must first be created in our lives; then out of the conviction of our own faith, it will be manifested. Everything that God is **going** to do for us He will first do **in** us. Nothing functions until our "spirit attitude" knows (has an intercourse experience) with His Spirit so that all indecisiveness or double-minded thoughts are removed. Only when we see what is already finished in the heavens, with the single eye of God, can we have the conviction of faith, the KNOWING, that surpasses ALL our natural understanding. When this posture is fixed, the move of God will be manifested in us and through us!

> *To release the supernatural into the world, we must first have a Divine unity of oneness between our thoughts and our heart, so that when our mouth speaks we choose LIFE.*

It is with this understanding that Jesus said, *"I am the light of the world: he that followeth me shall not walk in darkness, but shall have the light of life"* (John 8:12). Once we have the knowing that our life is His, we have the power and authority to BE, *"the light of the world. A city that is set on a hill cannot be hid"* (Matt. 5:14). *"God is love; and he that dwelleth in love dwelleth in God, and God in him. Herein is our love made perfect, that we may have boldness in the day of judgment* (when our adversary accuses us): *because as He is, so are we in this world"* (1 John 4:16-17).

Notes of reflection and meditation

What were your immediate thoughts as you read this chapter?

_____

_____

_____

_____

_____

_____

What seemed confusing from what you thought?

_____

_____

_____

_____

_____

_____

What was something new that you had not heard before?

_____

_____

_____

_____

_____

_____

CHAPTER 7

Divine Grace

As I was researching the scriptures that contain the word "grace" in the Strong's Concordance, I was intrigued to find that the word is not used in the books of Matthew and Mark. In Luke it is only used one time and in John three times. It is used sparingly in the Old Testament, and in abundance in the books from Acts to Revelation. The fact that it was rarely mentioned throughout the four gospels surprised me.

Throughout my Christian life I often heard the word "grace" in connection to salvation through Jesus Christ. I was also told that it was a gift from God that we did not deserve because we were sinners from the lineage of the first Adam. I was taught that because of His love, God extends grace to us. I also heard that He gave us free will, and if we don't accept His gift of grace we would spend eternity in hell.

I decided that I wanted to allow the Holy Spirit to teach me through the scriptures instead of relying on the knowledge of theologians. The Holy Spirit took me to Psalm 136:26, *"O give thanks unto the God of heaven: for his mercy endureth forever."* Then we went to Psalm 121: 5-8, *"The Lord is thy keeper: the Lord is thy shade upon thy right hand. The sun shall not smite thee by day, nor the moon by night. The Lord shall preserve thee from all evil: he shall preserve thy soul. The Lord shall preserve thy going out and thy coming in from this time forth, and even forevermore."* We then went into the New Testament to Luke 1:37, *"For with God nothing shall be impossible,"* and finally to Philippians 2:13, *"For it is God which worketh in you both to will and to do of his good pleasure."*

The Holy Spirit began to change my heart and mind to see that God's mercy does not have a time or limitations. It is forever; therefore, there can't be an eternal hell. Based on this information, I have realized that other areas of the Christian "doctrine" need reconsideration as well. Please consider the following thoughts (they will connect back to grace):

1. Nothing happens that God does not orchestrate. He has complete control of all. We are not puppets, but participants. God's sovereignty is not over us, but through us.

2. God is not interested in anyone's opinion about what He has done, but our obedience.

3. There is no such thing as free will, or being a free moral agent. Those are theological words that are not in scripture. We never had a say in when we were born, who our parents were, what race or color we wanted to be, what time in history we wanted to come into this world, whether we would be male or female, or when we would even die. We have no say in the plan or purpose of what God is doing.

4. Man is created in the image of God. He is not moral or free. We are the children of God and therefore must recognize our identity as such in order to do the Father's business on this earth. (John 17: 22-26)

5. Even though we do not have a free will, we do have a choice to live according to His purpose. Our choice is within His will which is His divine plan and purpose which will take place. We can disobey or violate the will of God, but not His purpose. If we obey His will we are part of the plan. If we disobey we forfeit to be a part, but the plan will move on to the next generation.

6. The word of God will not return void. It will travel through time and generations until the fulfillment of His divine plan is manifested.

7. God does not need us to reach the world. Many people are going out as missionaries, but are teaching God plus religion. God is looking for a company of people that are willing to be obedient to His purpose: To be the saviors on the earth (Obadiah 1:21).

So what is the truth behind GRACE?

Grace is the force of God; His eternal power. It means: unconditional kindness, unmerited favor, to bend or stoop down with no limitations of love for another.

Wherever sin exists, grace is more in abundance. Grace reigns...in LIFE.

Grace is an inheritance given to us when Jesus died on the cross over 2000 years ago.

When we know Jesus Christ by faith as our personal savior, we connect with the power and influence of this inheritance by fellowshipping with the Spirit of God. He causes us to see beyond our natural understanding of grace. We have a new method and kind of life which comes into our presence that continually reminds us that "nothing is impossible with God."

When we allow our life to be governed in time, we get relaxed with this power of grace and enter back into the methods of the world which include works. Grace then remains connected with salvation, but not with the reigning power of life and inheritance.

The word "grace" comes from the Greek word "charis" which means to be cheerful, comely, or well off. It was used by the Romans as a "wish you well" in departing from someone, but there was no power behind the words spoken. The Greeks used this word as "unearned favor" like giving a birthday gift or in saying a nice farewell to others.

The church took the word "grace" from the Romans to mean "we have received this "unearned favor" from God as a gift, not according to works that any should boast, but according to His love. With time, the church added to the word undeserved to the definition of grace. While unearned means you had nothing to do with receiving this gift of grace, undeserved means you get the opposite. Instead of the Father giving the gift of grace to His children, we are seen as unworthy animals that God is feeling sorry for, so He extends His grace. If we are not obedient to Him He will whip us liken to beating a dog.

If we try to apply grace with "unearned, undeserved favor" because we are sinners saved by grace, then there is a real problem in interpreting what Luke wrote about Jesus in 2:40, *"And the child grew, and waxed strong in spirit, filled with **wisdom**: and the **grace** of God was upon him"*.

Again, the Greeks used this word "grace" like you would say "I wish you happiness." It was a nice thought with no power. It was an empty word used to be nice. When God brought this word into His calling through Jesus Christ He filled the word "grace" or "charis" with power to carry out His wish (will) and desire.

We don't earn His "grace" or His will and desire. It is an inheritance given so that we can reign with the power of Life. The grace of God is a whole new kind of life. When God does something He always does it in abundance. There is never anything lacking.

DIVINE GRACE: It reigns completely, unmerited, unsought, all together unattached to anything outside of itself. There is nothing we can do to receive it. It cannot be bought, earned or won. The recipient has no claim upon it. It comes by complete charity, unasked for, undesired. The only requirement is the faith to believe because it is sovereign. Even the faith to believe has no claim by the recipient because it is the faith of God, not self.

Grace is Eternal – 2 Timothy 1:9
Grace is Free – Romans 3:24
Grace Reigns – Romans 5:21
Grace is foundational – Zech. 4:7

The reigning of God's grace chose you. It is the election of His grace, the ruler, and the sovereignty of His grace which chose us before the fall of the first Adam. We are justified freely through grace (Romans 3:24). There is NO cause involved. We have done NOTHING because He is the cause of pure sovereignty. We have all been chosen to receive this amazing, abundant grace.

There is a generation that will break the curse of death and it will begin with identifying with the power of God's divine grace. Just because death isn't being broken the way our natural mind thinks does not mean it hasn't been happening the way God intended. Examples: Noah never experienced rain and never before saw a boat. God decided to have a baby through a virgin.

Divine Grace is within each of us now, but we can only connect with it through our identity in Jesus Christ. When we acknowledge and walk in the truth that *"as He is so are we in this world"* (1 John 4: 17), divine grace is manifested from us to others drawing them to their heavenly Father.

"That they all may be one; as thou, Father, art in me, and I in thee, that they also may be one in us; that the world may believe that thou hast sent me" (John 17: 21).

Notes of reflection and meditation

What were your immediate thoughts as you read this chapter?

_____

_____

_____

_____

_____

_____

What seemed confusing from what you thought?

_____

_____

_____

_____

_____

What was something new that you had not heard before?

_____

_____

_____

_____

_____

_____

CHAPTER 8

Light and Energy
Luke 22

The hurricanes, storms, and earthquakes are cries of humanity. With life, there is responsibility. You do not just leave a baby at the hospital and come back later. The earth is crying for the sons of God to come forth.

The real issue that is going on in the earth is life and death. When we die, not all the riches matter

Verse 53: "power of darkness" (Strong's 4655). To deal with the darkness they went to the High priest (church) of the day where God was suppose to be known, experienced, and exalted. Instead, they mocked him, slapped him, and beat him (Jesus). When they blindfolded Him, they wanted Him to prophesy.

In Genesis 3 Adam and Eve had just eaten of the fruit. Their eyes were opened and they knew they were naked. They were operating out of what their senses knew as truth, but not truth.

Before the fall, Adam saw himself; He did not see a woman's body. They were both God Adam. After, they both changed because they were seeing with their natural eyes instead of their true identity. Before this time, Adam was naming everything out of His God identity. After, He continues naming, but now after his natural identity. He called Eve "the Mother of all living." Mother in the Strong's Concordance is "EM."

"EM" stands for energy x mass (matter) over "c," they see differently. Jesus' eyes were blind. E = energy, M = matter for all living. They did not see the way they use to. When we have "c", we have Light (speed of light). The relationship between energy and matter can be exchanged. Energy is neither created nor destroyed. It can be changed into matter, but not destroyed.

An atomic bomb can be changed matter into energy. You can see how much matter can be changed into how much energy. All matter has energy in it. That is what holds it together. The energy keeps the matter together. Adam was saying, but not seeing. Adam was saying, "Let there be light," but he was not seeing it with spiritual eyes.

Mother (EM) means the parting of the ways. The way of Light, the power and energy of Light, departed from them. Jesus came and said, *"I am the way, the truth, and the Life"* (John 14:16). He is the "c" for LIGHT.

An atom is split apart to get energy. Adam was split so that Light could come in. Once they see that the energy of light is in the atom, they realize that it has to be split to get to the light.

Total energy of the world is constant. You cannot destroy or create matter. I am the Lord God I change not. Light is a constant. It is one speed in a vacuum. It never changes. It is the same 1000 years ago as it is today. Just because we do not see, it does not mean it is not real. Jesus said we are the Light of the world. The human body emulates light sending out an electrical field around it that we cannot see with our natural eyes, but can be picked up by a camera. It is not a religion, but a fact that we are light beings that never change.

Eve is the source of all life. E= MC (2). Energy = Matter (human) x Light (heaven forces). When the "c" or light is in place, there is power and energy. It takes many Atoms to create an atomic bomb.

An atom is made of a trinity of: Protons, electrons, and neutrons. Light has a trinity also:

Eve had the energy and matter, but not the light to see. The light is there, but not turned on.

Time ended over 2000 years ago. God covered Adam and Eve with skin. Moses and Elijah brought the Word to Life on this earth. Moses demonstrated a power greater than anything did that had occurred on the earth before. When the Light and Moses became one, He shined to a point that He had to have his face veiled. Adam and Eve could not SEE any longer.

All birth starts with LIGHT. The difference between a believer and non-believer is that they cannot see. Jesus took blindness upon Himself in Luke 22 so that all humankind could see

EMC = LIFE. Let your Light shine so that men will know your god identity.
Energy + Mass = Light

God did not change Adam. When a skin (flesh) was put on them (male and femal), they no longer could see the way they did before. They looked through eyes of inferior (natural) understanding based on their flesh. We are LIGHT BEINGS today. In the fullness of time (over 2000 years ago), everything was made NEW. Religion and the media do not see God, which is why they are in darkness. When we see Him through the unveiling of the Holy Spirit, all power and all authority come forth. When Jesus stood in front of the religious system, they did not see God which is why they were powerless and in darkness.

The only reason we are not seeing changes in the earth today is that our "god" eyes, given to us by the Holy Spirit when we received Jesus as our Lord, and our natural mouths do not agree.

When the atomic bomb was made, it is because a series of atoms had to be brought together. For transformation to be seen in the earth, the sons of God must come together in unity of the faith and see with the eyes of God. We have to say it the way the Bible tells us and believe that it is truth. We have to agree with Scripture to change the world, not to focus on our personal gain such as healing or prosperity. It is not about one person, but a corporate body of Christ.

Paul tells us, *"For he, Jesus Christ, is our peace, who hath made both one, and hath broken down the middle wall of partition between us; Having abolished in his flesh the enmity, even the law of commandments contained in ordinances; for to make in himself of twain one new man, so making peace; And that he might reconcile both unto God in one body by the cross, having slain the enmity thereby"* (Ephesians 2:14-16 KJV).

Lot is an example of being a son of God, but rather than changing the city, He conformed to the life of the city that was living in darkness. We know this because he had married daughters that were still virgins.

When Adam called his wife's name Eve because she was the mother of all living, she had the energy and matter. God changes not. People that are in darkness are not seeing what God sees which is in them. Man looks at the flesh, but God looks at the heart. Man looks at the logic and reason, but God looks at the spirit. What spirit is talking and functioning in our body?

"For we wrestle not against flesh and blood, but against principalities, against powers, against the rulers of the darkness of this world, against spiritual wickedness in high places" (Ephesians 6:12).

God covered humankind with skin. We now have the same kind people as Moses and Elijah were on the mount of transfiguration. In fact, the same as Jesus was. Moses and Elijah brought the word to life. Moses demonstrated a power that was greater than any power that was on the earth. The light and Moses became one. God did not destroy Adam and Eve. They just could not see any more the way God sees. The fruit of the Tree of Knowledge of Good and Evil caused them to where they were not able to see Truth and Life any longer, which brought in death into existence. They could not SEE any longer.

The only difference between a Christian and a non-believer is they cannot see what is already before them. However, those claiming to be Christians should be seeing the Light of the Word meaning that the blood of Jesus has set all humankind free crucified over 2000 years ago. This is the good news of the gospel. Our salvation through Jesus Christ was always meant to be SOZO, saved, healed, and delivered spirit, soul, and body while in the earth as a member, or cell, of the one new man Christ Jesus.

If we are not seeing the way God sees, we will die. Jesus demonstrated this death when he allowed himself to be blindfolded, taking part in the natural death that was a part of every person.

Light =EMC (square). Energy + Mass seeing through God's eyes = LIGHT

Let your light shine so humanity will know your godliness and theirs.

Adam and Eve no longer saw themselves the way God saw them. They were the same, but could not see through spiritual eyes. Adam did not believe that he was the god identity that God had made him. He was already a son of God on this earth before he ate of the Tree of Knowledge.

When Jesus stood in front of the religious system of the day, they did not see God. They were seeing with their natural eyes instead of spiritual. The only reason we are not seeing the earth change is that our mouths must line up with our spiritual eyes. The reason we agree with the word of God is to change the world, not ourselves that we already believe that we are changed. Healing and prosperity will automatically change when we believe for others according to the Word.

When the priest went in the house of God, they could not be blind, or have any aliments. They had to be LIGHT, which means they could SEE with God eyes to transform matter and energy into His image (Leviticus 21:18).

In verse 22:22 of Leviticus; blind, broken, or wounded could not be offered to God. These animals represented the people. True blindness is not physical blindness, but not seeing with spiritual eyes the way God sees. Jesus allowed himself to be blindfolded so we could be redeemed to see with our god eyes. Jesus was blinded physically by natural man demanding that He prophesy with His natural eyes covered. True prophesy has nothing to do with our natural eyes. It is with spiritual eyes that brings prophesies of God. Today, the church still evaluates truth by what they see with their natural eyes.

In ancient days, men that were blind were sought out and well paid as guards over the entrances to the underground water gates of the city. They didn't need their sight, and their other senses were usually above average to move around caves easily.

(Reference in Deuteronomy 15:21 with animals being offered to God: If they were lame or blind, they could not be offered.)

Deuteronomy 28: 28

"The Lord shall smite thee with madness and blindness and astonishment of heart and thou shalt grope at noon day as a blind groper in darkness." This darkness speaks of death. This is not the darkness of Genesis 1:2. The Lord shall smite these people. The Lord saw them as Light, but they were bringing in sacrifices of a false identity other than Light Beings. They did not become darkness, but were LIGHT covered with blindness.

Deuteronomy 8:3

"And he humbled thee, and suffered thee to hunger, and fed thee with manna, which thou knewest not, neither did thy fathers know; that he might make thee know that man doth not live by bread only, but by every word that proceedeth out of the mouth of the LORD doth man live."

Proverbs 14:15

"The simple believeth every word: but the prudent man looketh well to his going."

Proverbs 30:5

"Every word of God is pure: he is a shield unto them that put their trust in him."

Matthew 4:4

"But he answered and said, it is written, Man shall not live by bread alone, but by every word that proceedeth out of the mouth of God."

Matthew 18:16

But if he will not hear thee, then take with thee one or two more, that in the mouth of two or three witnesses every word may be established.

Luke 4:4

"And Jesus answered him, saying, it is written, that man shall not live by bread alone, but by every word of God."

2 Corinthians 13:1

"This is the third time I am coming to you. In the mouth of two or three witnesses shall every word be established."

2 Samuel 5: 6-10:

Jerusalem speaks of the Holy City. The blind and lamb cannot come into the city of David. It is not God that causes world issues, but the imagination of humankind that has the ability to create darkness around them. God did not kill Adam and Eve. Adam that brought death into existence and it is his seed that has brought every horrible thing on this earth. Jesus came and reversed the system, making all humankind new creatures in Christ, but without seeing through our Christ eyes, we limit the power for transformation to take place.

We now have all energy and all power because we possess the Light that assures us that we have the power to change. It is not an ego thing or psychic power, but all God; Light and Truth in us being manifested out of us.

Do you believe the Word of God?

Psalm 146:8:

"The LORD openeth the eyes of the blind: the LORD raiseth them that are bowed down: the LORD loveth the righteous." The Lord reveals to us that we are already righteousness of God. Abraham could not say he was righteous until God revealed this to him in Gen 17.

Isaiah 29:18:

"And in that day shall the deaf hear the words of the book, and the eyes of the blind shall see out of obscurity, and out of darkness." This day was when Jesus rose from the grave. The darkness is (Strong's 2822), referring to darkness of spirit and the grave.

Isaiah 35:4:

"Say to them that are of a fearful heart, be strong, and fear not: behold, your God will come with vengeance, even God with recompense; he will come and save you." God is salvation.

Isaiah 35:5:

"Then the eyes of the blind shall be opened, and the ears of the deaf shall be unstopped."

Isaiah 49:5:

"And now, saith the LORD that formed me from the womb to be his servant, to bring Jacob again to him, though Israel be not gathered, yet shall I be glorious in the eyes of the LORD, and my God shall be my strength."

In Genesis Chapter 17, Abram illustrates an understanding of God being his father when God came through the blood and raised Abram to a higher level that he could not do himself. In Ch. 22, Abram is ready for his real identity and had his name changed to Abraham.

The water became clouded afterwards. It was this water that Moses came out of as a baby into Egypt searching for a father and not wanting to settle for a stepfather.

Genesis is the beginning of the water of the word: 1:1-3 = mass, energy, and light.

Jesus went up = came out of the water differently. He heard the voice in the heavens within himself.
When Jesus went to the wedding, he called his mother woman = Adam.

John 3:17:

"For God sent not his Son into the world to condemn the world; but that the world through him might be saved."

John 3:18:

"He that believeth on him is not condemned: but he that believeth not is condemned already, because he hath not believed in the name of the only begotten Son of God."

Galatians 3:26-29:

"We are the source of being baptized in - Christ. We must see ourselves the way the Bible says who we are. We are condemned already when we say we are Christians, but allow the world to be our view of the way things are."

Galatians 3:26:

"For ye are all the children of God by faith in Christ Jesus."

Galatians 4:6:

"And because ye are sons, God hath sent forth the Spirit of his Son into your hearts, crying, Abba, Father."

Isaiah 43:1

"But now thus saith the LORD that created thee, O Jacob, and he that formed thee, O Israel, Fear not: for I have redeemed thee, I have called thee by thy name; thou art mine." Jesus had not even come to earth yet. When Adam and Eve were sent out of the garden, redemption was already there, but that had to SEE it.

Galatians 4:7

"Wherefore thou art no more a servant, but a son; and if a son, then an heir of God through Christ." Being an heir of God is our god identity of who we really are today.

We must know ourselves as God knows us. God is not the destroyer, but the maker of every good thing.

May we know the revelation, which causes us to be aware physically of the identity that we possess, which incorporates completeness and wholeness of our identity in God.

Notes of reflection and meditation

What were your immediate thoughts as you read this chapter?

_____

_____

_____

_____

_____

_____

What seemed confusing from what you thought?

_____

_____

_____

_____

_____

_____

What was something new that you had not heard before?

_____

_____

_____

_____

_____

_____

CHAPTER 9

The Mystery of Blindness

"For I would not, brethren, that ye should be ignorant of this mystery, lest ye should be wise in your own conceits; that blindness in part is happened to Israel, until the fullness of the Gentiles be come in. And so all Israel shall be saved: as it is written, There shall come out of Zion the Deliverer, and shall turn away ungodliness from Jacob: For this is my covenant unto them, when I shall take away their sins. As concerning the gospel, they are enemies for your sakes: but as touching the election, they are beloved for the Fathers' sakes. For the gifts and calling of God are without repentance. For as ye in times past have not believed God, yet have now obtained mercy through their unbelief: Even so have these also now not believed, that through your mercy they also may obtain mercy. For God hath concluded them all in unbelief, that he might have mercy upon all" Romans 11:25-32.

The purpose of a mystery is to cause us to dig and unveil something we did not know or understand before. It may be a mystery when we started searching, but we are also meant to find what we are looking for. Most churches today take what has been given to us by God as a mystery and placed it on a shelf rather than searching out a deeper relationship with God and His understanding.

Another reason for a mystery is to provoke us to go beyond our comfort zone. *"We may not all sleep, but we will all be changed,"* willing or unwilling, we will all be changed (1 Corinthians 15:51). If someone brings a truth that challenges our mind, it should put our natural understanding into over load causing the Holy Spirit to step in and take over. However, many of those that consider themselves Christians live as a "homosectarian" meaning that if a person is not of the same doctrine understanding about the Scriptures or believing with the same denominational bondage, they do not want to be a part of their fellowship. They seek justification many times through teachings or educational degrees passed down through generations and traditions. "Whose commentary are you using, or what school did you go to?" This is often the direction justification will go to seek out authenticity of man versus hearing from the Holy Spirit.

Paul has written to the Christians in Rome that partial blindness has come to some people's natural understanding (Israel) until the fullness of the Gentiles took place. Some people simply will not understand the mystery of God because He has purposely placed blindness to their understanding. This blindness is for the sake of those that do understand the Scriptures with the mind of Christ to bring all humankind to the Father. Difficulty comes when the blindness is on someone very close to you making a wedge in the relationship in order to come to a mutual understanding of God's word. When this happens, only the Holy Spirit can remove the wedge that was established with the unconditional love of God found in at least one person's heart of the party. It is the unconditional kindness of our Christ identity, which will cause a reaction to the wedge.

The Gospel of Christ was hidden for OUR sake. If Israel had understood the completeness of what God did on Calvary, we may not have the Gospel today. History shows us that when we look at other religions we still see the predominance of certain countries with that particular religion. With the Gospel of Christ given to the Gentiles, Christianity has spread all over the world infiltrating into cultures, nations, and religions today.

For Americans, the Bible is viewed as the Holy Word of God, but in other countries, it may be just another book. To share an understanding about Christ to those in countries outside the United States who are predominately of another religion takes more than just using a Bible. It takes the unction of the Holy Spirit to communicate on their level of understanding producing signs and wonders (2 Corinthians 12:12). The first sign and wonder that they will question is when the unconditional love of God is presented to them. No judgment or condemnation, but the kind of hug and smile to a stranger that speaks with no words "your special." This is a foreign gesture not shared even among their own people in other religions.

God is not bound by any limits with His ability to bless; however, we have placed limitation on what we allow ourselves to receive with a veil of justification. God has given us His understanding of His ways by the Holy Spirit so that those who receive it would give His unconditional love and mercy away to others. It is easy to love those that are kind and loving to you, but it takes the Spirit of God to love and bless unconditionally those that curse you slandering your name and character.

God is aware that some people will not give His mercy away, but keep it for themselves. These people are at peace about their own salvation while judging others to a place they refer to as "hell." What they do not understand is that the body of Christ is one body. Jesus completed a mission that came for the whole body. Therefore, if we blasphemy someone with judgment or condemnation in our mind, our "heaven" is not obtainable until we release unconditional mercy and love seeing them as part of the same body. We are actually hurting ourselves when we think anything less than blessing someone else.

Look around you and see the diversity in nature with oceans, the forest, the mountains, and the fields. There is so much variety of life in each of these areas yet if something is taken out; it throws off the balance and beauty of what God created. He created diversity for flavor loving the uniqueness of each of us. He was the one who cut off natural understanding as an enemy of the Gospel, but He also said they are beloved for His sake.

The ways of God are not the ways of our intellectual understanding.

God has not changed His mind about non-believers, but gave the message of unconditional love, mercy, and grace to those that He knew would give it away without justification. These believers have come through over-coming areas in their life accepting the child-like faith of knowing that God is in control, and He is all and in ALL.

Let us read **Colossians 1:12-22**

"Giving thanks unto the Father, which hath made us meet to be partakers of the inheritance of the saints in light: Who hath delivered us from the power of darkness, and hath translated us into the kingdom of his dear Son: In whom we have redemption through his blood, even the forgiveness of sins: Who is the image of the invisible God, the firstborn of every creature: For by him were all things created, that are in heaven, and that are in earth, visible and invisible, whether they be thrones, or dominions, or principalities, or powers: all things were created by him, and for him: And he is before all things, and by him all things consist. And he is the head of the body, the church: who is the beginning, the firstborn from the dead; that in all things he might have the preeminence. For it pleased the Father that in him should all fullness dwell; And, having made peace through the blood of his cross, by him to reconcile all things unto himself; by him, I say, whether they be things in earth, or things in heaven. And you, that were

*sometime alienated and enemies in your mind by wicked works, **yet now** hath he reconciled in the body of his flesh through death, to present you holy and unblameable and unreproveable in his sight:"*

Paul is telling us in the verses that everything is finished before God. Take note of these words: *"all, fullness, hath, things, made peace, earth, heaven, yet now, and reconciled"* that Paul wrote and ask yourself if they really mean what they say, and does this understanding fit into the doctrine of Christianity that has been taught in many of our churches in America? Does our understanding apply towards other countries?

The realm of Judaism has a spirit of inclusiveness to be better than others. They still consider themselves the chosen ones. God has given them this spirit. As Gentiles, we had the identity of being sons of God, but not the access to come into the understanding of our identity in Him until we were "grafted" into the vine by the blood of Jesus. Before that, we were alienated and lost to the understanding that God is our Heavenly Father also. Only through Jesus do we have access to a "family relationship" with God.

The word "grafted" was made into a legalistic doctrine holding the body of Christ hostage to what Paul was saying. The Gentiles are not people who now have the ability to choose God to be their adopted Father, yet have a different bloodline with a different DNA from the Jews. There is no evidence in nature where a child can choose his biological parents. Another family may adopt a child, but they cannot change the bloodline inheritance they received from their parents. We were **all**, both Jews and Gentiles, originated from Adam who was a son of God (Luke 3:38).

Jews knew of their identity, which we have recorded in the Old Testament. They preserved the Hebrew heritage by keeping the teachings of God through the Torah. Through the ages of time and history in the Christian church we have identified the Jews, the land of Israel, and the Torah as one. We have given them the totality of inheritance given to Abraham separating ourselves and beliefs that they are from Moses and believers in Christ we identify as Gentiles are now identified with Jesus.

During the era of when Jesus walked on the earth, the Jews felt they had a closer relationship with God, not passing this knowledge and relationship on to the Gentiles, but lifted themselves up as being "holier than thou" and using their identity to control others. They belittled the rest of humanity as not being quite good enough, so God blinded their understanding and released the fullness of His love and mercy to the rest of the world through the shedding of the blood of Jesus Christ who is the High Priest for all humankind. In so doing, the Gentiles who now have the Gospel are not to be "homosectarians" by treating others as the Jews did, but to take the Father's unconditional love and release it on those who were blinded for OUR sake.

God has turned the lights off on some people so that His LIGHT would come on in others to take the Gospel to the ends of the world. Blindness is only temporary. We must stop trying to change people from who they were into whom we believe a Christian is supposed to be making us all alike. God loves diversity and His body is made of many members that **work together in love as one body.** There is no difference to God between cultures or doctrines. We are not to make converts but disciples.

On the other side of the history journey, much of today's body of believers in Christ Jesus have allowed their own limitations of receiving the fullness of their inheritance in Christ because of the teachings of the church about being a gentile or pagan. The word gentile in the Scriptures was not meant to be a separate bloodline, but those within the bloodline that had become worldly and caught up in the life style and cultures or the Greeks and Romans.

In the Old Testament, after Solomon's son became king, the northern tribes and southern tribes split. The southern tribes originating from Jacob's sons where made of the tribes of Judah, Benjamin, and half of Levi. The northern tribes were the other 10 sons. The tribe of Levi was not

> *Southern tribes were Judah, Benjamin, and half of Levi. Today, these are all known as the Jews.*

given any territory on either the northern or southern areas allocated by God to Joshua at Shechem found in the writings of Moses in Deuteronomy.

During the Babylonian captivity around 700BC when Nebuchadnezzar captured the northern tribes they scattered all over what we know today as Europe and taking on the culture, religions, and customs of those lands. The southern tribes went through a similar captivity about 200 years later. The northern tribes became known as the 10 lost tribes. The southern tribes became known as the Jews since the tribe of Judah was the largest of the southern tribes. Many of the southern tribes of Judah came back in the documentation we have in Ezra and Nehemiah to rebuild Jerusalem. They also had the heart desire to reestablish the Torah teachings of Moses.

> *The northern tribes were: Reuben, Simeon, Issachar, Asher, Dan, Zebulon, Gad, Naphtali, (Joseph's sons) Ephraim, Manasseh, and half the tribe of Levi. Ephraim was the largest tribe, so the northern tribes together were known as Ephramites and/or Israel. These are the Gentiles in the New Testament.*

Blindness is only for a season until the fullness of the Gentiles. The reason the fullness has not been manifested after over 2000 years is that the church still wants to separate and divide the body of Christ with justification. Once we understand of the ways of God, He will remove the blindness from others. We will not need to bring fear, condemnation, or force-feed anyone with the Gospel because the unconditional love of God flowing through us is the greatest power to overcome darkness. If we can just understand, that God loves ALL and we have a responsibility to do the same. It is not our responsibility to win the whole world to Christ; Jesus has already won the battle. It is our responsibility to show people their heavenly Father and how much He loved us while we were in darkness and ignorance to the understanding of His great love (Romans 5:8).

"For the gifts and calling of God are without repentance" (Romans 11:29). Our salvation is a FREE gift from God. God cannot take it back or change His mind. He has given it to the world and has covenant with Himself to bring all creation to Himself that He is all in ALL. If we believe and share His identity by being a son of God doing the Father's business as Jesus showed us, He will remove the blinders on others. Christians are to look like Him, as He looks like all men to believers. We do not need a 12-step plan to reach people, but believe that He will do it through us when we reach out to others with the Spirit of God being manifested.

Key factors to understanding the mystery of blindness:

- Blindness in part will come to those that God veils their understanding until the fullness of the Gentiles.
- All Israel (humankind) shall be saved.
- Unbelievers are enemies of the Gospel for the sake of BELIEVERS.
- Unbelievers are loved for the Father's sake.
- Unbelievers obtain mercy through the unconditional mercy of believers that the Father revealed to them.
- God concluded all in unbelief that He would have mercy upon ALL.

Believers only received mercy from God because the Jews and unbelievers did not understand the ways of God; not because we believed. Unbelievers now receive mercy because we give it to them from the understanding of the fullness of His great love that He has for all humanity and us. Please re-read Romans Chapter Eleven asking the Holy Spirit to unveil any blindness you may have to the fullness of our Father's love.

Jesus said, "I am not sent but unto the lost sheep of the house of Israel." (Matthew 15:24). The lost sheep are the whole house of Israel, the linage of all of Jacob's sons, not just the Jews.

"For with God nothing shall be impossible" (Luke 1:37).

Notes of reflection and meditation

What were your immediate thoughts as you read this chapter?

_____

_____

_____

_____

_____

_____

What seemed confusing from what you thought?

_____

_____

_____

_____

_____

_____

What was something new that you had not heard before?

_____

_____

_____

_____

_____

_____

CHAPTER 10

Mystery of Christ

"For this cause I Paul, the prisoner of Jesus Christ for you Gentiles, If ye have heard of the dispensation of the grace of God which is given me to you ward: How that by revelation he made known unto me the mystery; (as I wrote afore in few words, Whereby, when ye read, ye may understand my knowledge in the mystery of Christ) Which in other ages was not made known unto the sons of men, as it is now revealed unto his holy apostles and prophets by the Spirit; That the Gentiles should be fellow heirs, and of the same body, and partakers of his promise in Christ by the gospel: Whereof I was made a minister, according to the gift of the grace of God given unto me by the effectual working of his power. Unto me, who am less than the least of all saints, is this grace given, that I should preach among the Gentiles the unsearchable riches of Christ; And to make all men see what is the fellowship of the mystery, which from the beginning of the world hath been hid in God, who created all things by Jesus Christ: To the intent that now unto the principalities and powers in heavenly places might be known by the church the manifold wisdom of God, According to the eternal purpose which he purposed

in Christ Jesus our Lord: In whom we have boldness and access with confidence by the faith of him" (Ephesians 3:1-12).

God is not playing hide and seek to confuse us, but has placed mysteries in Scripture for our growth and development. Mysteries are not for confusion, however, for us to get a hunger to understand the ways of God.

There are twenty-seven times the word "mystery" is used in the New Testament. Twenty of them are generic; not connected with any particular mystery. However, seven of them are specific such as "the mystery of Christ" found in Ephesians 3:4.

Some of the things to consider when solving a mystery that came from God are that studying is necessary; however, it takes the revelation of God for us to discern the mystery. What God has veiled comes to us when we go boldly before the throne and ask for it. To understand what is written in any writing, we must know the heart and intent of the author. When we know the author (character and nature) then we can receive revelation of the one who wrote the book.

God will often offend our mind to reveal our heart. Most of the time we are either locked up in the past or liberating the future. When God puts demands, which push us into a place where our natural mind cannot understand, rather than accepting what the Holy Spirit is revealing to us with a teachable spirit, we usually try to justify, analyze, or compromise what God is doing.

Father God loves to spend quality time with His children tossing His words back and forth to see how we play.

In the culture of the Old Testament, learning phases were a four part step with the Rabbi's teachings. As a little child wisdom was given straightforward or literal. As a school age child wisdom was taught with reference of the past to go forward. As a young adult wisdom was taught with discussions of sharing each other's thoughts and answering questions by asking a question. The last phase was a self-relationship with the Father and using all the wisdom, teachings, and meditations to hear the Holy Spirit unveil the treasures of Heaven to be released in the earth as the Kingdom of God. Most believers in Christ are functioning in their Christian life as a little child, even though they may have been believers in Jesus Christ with Ph.D. in theology for many years.

The majority of humankind does not like change. It is something that is never easy, but always necessary. Many times, we have to get to the point of suffocating or choking with DIS-EASE that surrounds us before we are willing to move in the direction and wisdom God has for us.

Paul teaches us in Ephesians that the spiritual significance of the mysteries that God refers to in Scripture comes to us by the Spirit of God witnessing to our spirit. It is not known by the intellect of man, but by sons of God. The standard of the ways of God are not enforced by law, but by revelation. When the love of God comes by revelation, we do not want to do the old ways. We must allow the fullness and power of the love of God to be in control instead of mixing grace with law.

God is not a dispensationalist. The only dispensation that Paul embraces is GRACE. A dispensationalist says, "There is a moment in time and season for something to happen that God planned to happen," however, this does not line up with the character and nature of who God is. His way is to work in covenant agreement with His people, not dispensationalist. He does not work with the restrains of time, but the power of agreement in covenant. Again, LAW AND GRACE DO NOT MIX, but Grace and the teachings and instructions of God do.

God does not come at any time, but in the fullness of time when the Spirit and Bride come into agreement. Everything God has promised in scripture we have NOW. He is not moved by our needs or emotions, but by covenant and our action.

The Mystery of Christ takes us from having nothing, into being heirs of God with every promise that has been made by the Father. To release this mystery we must plant a seed by taking what little we THINK we have and giving it away. This is what gets God's attention to move in our lives, not the begging and pleading with God through our prayers.

In Genesis 6:3, we read, *"And the LORD said, my spirit shall not always strive with man, for that he also is flesh: yet his days shall be an hundred and twenty years."*

Many who were in a position to reveal the love of God as Father, but instead brought fear and condemnation to His people have used this verse. It is the kindness and love of God that leads men to repentance. God will not always have an issue of blood with man for grace will prevail through flesh "for that He also is flesh" drawing all men to Him for He is All in All.

GOD HAS NOT BEEN ANGRY WITH MAN SINCE CALVARY. JESUS CHRIST MADE PEACE WITH GOD AND HIS CREATION AS ADAM (1 Corinthians 15).

The number, one-hundred and twenty, is the number of Pentecost. Pryor to this time in Acts 2 man was flesh, but now he is spirit (Romans 8:9). The Holy Spirit is in each of us declaring us the sons of God. *"Behold the Lamb of God, which taketh away the SIN of the world."* (John 1:29)

In Luke 3:4-6 we read, "As is written in the book of the words of Isaiah the prophet:

> *"A voice of one calling in the desert,*
> *'Prepare the way for the Lord,*
> *make straight paths for him.*
> *Every valley shall be filled in,*
> *every mountain and hill made low.*
> *The crooked roads shall become straight,*
> *the rough ways smooth.*
> **And all mankind will see God's salvation.**" NIV

Therefore, what have we learned from Paul about the Mystery of Christ in Ephesians Chapter Three?

- This mystery becomes enlightened to us by revelation, not Old Testament understanding (vs. 3).
- The sons of men in the Old Testament did not know this mystery. It was made manifest to the sons of God by the Holy Spirit through Calvary and the resurrection of Jesus Christ (vs. 5).
- The Gentiles are fellow heirs with the people of God in the Old Testament. Today, they have the same promises as the Jewish people (vs. 6).
- The Old Testament prophets joined with the New Testament Apostles by revelation of the Holy Spirit making known the mystery of fellowship (vs. 5).
- ALL things were created by Christ (vs. 9).
- The mysteries of God will be revealed through the church. *"To the disciple, Behold thy mother"* (John 19:27). When we walk into son ship, we do not disregard the church. The woman will always be important to the heart of God (vs. 10).

I close with a few lines from a poem by Terri McPherson Buckley titled *"You are a Miracle"*:

> *You are a child of Creation*
> *A reflection of God*
> *No on can steal your beauty*
> *Unless you let them*
> *Don't let them*
> *You are a miracle of God's love*
> *God's Love!*
> *A Miracle!*

Notes of reflection and meditation

What were your immediate thoughts as you read this chapter?

_____
_____
_____
_____
_____
_____

What seemed confusing from what you thought?

_____
_____
_____
_____
_____
_____

What was something new that you had not heard before?

_____
_____
_____
_____
_____
_____

CHAPTER 11

The Mystery of God:
Christ is in You

"Whereof I am made a minister, according to the dispensation of God which is given to me for you, to fulfill the word of God; Even the mystery which hath been hid from ages and from generations, but now is made manifest to his saints: To whom God would make known what is the riches of the glory of this mystery among the Gentiles; which is Christ in you, the hope of glory: Whom we preach, warning every man, and teaching every man in all wisdom; that we may present every man perfect in Christ Jesus" (Colossians 1:25-28).

The mystery that is being revealed to the body of Christ is that God would take the fullness of Him and place it in each of person; not just theologians, or "you," but that Christ has been distributed evenly, and in all of us with the fullness of God. We need to clean up our lives so that Christ in us

"Here O Israel, the Lord thy God is one God"

Deuteronomy 6:4

can shine through us; not so we can place Christ in us. He is already there.

A partial truth that most Christians live by is: The Father is the creator; Jesus Christ is the redeemer; and the Holy Spirit is the enabler. The reality of this message is that God did not divide us up and say "one third" of the Godhead is in you. In other words; when we have Christ in us we did not just receive Jesus or just the Holy Spirit, but we have the fullness of the Godhead: Father, Son, and Holy Spirit is Christ. The word "Christ" is not Jesus' last name. Christ means the anointed on of the Godhead which is the fullness of God moving inside human vessels.

We are not individually "all of God," but all of God is within all of humankind. This is why we need each person for the fullness to be manifested. Isaiah 53:10-11 tells us, *"Yet it pleased the LORD to bruise him; he hath put him to grief: when thou shalt make his soul an offering for sin, he shall see his seed, he shall prolong his days, and the pleasure of the LORD shall prosper in his hand. He shall see of the travail of his soul, and shall be satisfied: by his knowledge shall my righteous servant justify many; for he shall bear their iniquities."*

The mystery of God IS: Everything that God is and will ever do with each of us is within us now. *"If a man love me, he will keep my words: and my Father will love him, and we will come unto him, and make our abode with him"* (John 14:23). The mystery is the completeness of Christ, not the undone Adam. In Colossians 1:28 when Paul says, *"Whom we preach, warning every man, and teaching every man in all wisdom; that we may present every man perfect in Christ Jesus."* he is not speaking of going to an eternal hell, but teaching in ALL wisdom presenting every man perfect and complete in Christ Jesus.

Jesus Christ said, "It is Finished." He then gave us the Holy Spirit to develop His body, the church, as He is so He would have a place to rest His head, Selah!

Jesus Christ has paid the price for ALL. If we do not believe this then we cannot believe that His life was enough to pay the penalty for sin and He has to come back to finish the job. Paul tells us in 2 Corinthians 5:15-21, *"And that he died for **all**, that they which live should not henceforth live unto themselves, but unto him which died for them, and rose again. Wherefore henceforth know we no man after the flesh: yea, though we have known Christ after the flesh, **yet now** henceforth know we him no more. Therefore if any man be in Christ, he is a new creature: old things are passed away; behold, **all things are become new**. And all things are of God, who hath reconciled us to himself by Jesus Christ, and hath given to us the ministry of reconciliation; To wit, that God was in Christ, reconciling the world unto himself, not imputing their trespasses unto them; and hath committed unto us the word of reconciliation. Now then we are ambassadors for Christ, as though God did beseech you by us: we pray you in Christ's stead, be ye reconciled to God. For he hath made him to be sin for us, who knew no sin; that we might be made the righteousness of God in him."*

Isaiah 53 told us that God's wrath had been removed, yet we insist that He wants to "get people" through justification, they find in Scripture. God judges no one, but gave all judgment to Jesus who paid the price (read John 5). If the price of sin has been paid for the world, whom are we to keep classifying people as being sinners? We have not removed our anger with humankind. Jesus was the first of a new convent breed that was capitally punished, falsely charged beyond recognition. Jesus not only took away sin from us; He took away the ability to offend our Heavenly Father.

When the body of Christ understands this by acknowledging all men perfect in Christ by faith, they will realize the power of unconditional love versus hate. We shortchange this great power of love that is within each of us trying to rationalize our understanding by mixing it with justification. The love of God will overcome all obstacles because it is His character and identity; not just a free gift of grace. *"And having* (unconditional love*) a readiness to revenge all disobedience, when* *your obedience* (unconditional love) *is fulfilled. Do ye look on things after the outward appearance? If any man trust to himself that he is Christ's, let him of himself think this again, that, as he is Christ's, even so are we* (all mankind) *Christ's"* 2 Corinthians 10:6-7.

God does not need to control us, but gave us guidelines that will help us make choices so we do not suffer hurtful consequences. However, if we do make the wrong choice, god is not out to tear us down even more, but to love us through the sowing and reaping of the consequence. What we sow we will reap which are built into the laws of nature that God provided for us. The bad seed we may sow does not change our identity of being children of God, but it does put a bondage that hinders us from having a quality relationship with God as mature in Christ. As long as we stay as a "child" in Christ, we continue to be more concerned with ourselves than about others. Being sons of God requires us to see the unity of the body of Christ as one. If someone falls short (body, soul, and/ or in spirit) of understanding how much God loves them, it is a son of God who covers that person with the unconditional love of God without judgment or condemnation. When that person comes into the presence of this kind of love, they experience a relationship with their Heavenly Father through you. It is not about us, but about doing the Father's business as Jesus did so that only the Father receives glory and honor.

Paul writes in his letter in Ephesians 1:3-4,*"Blessed be the God and Father of our Lord Jesus Christ, who **hath** blessed us with **all** spiritual blessings in heavenly places in Christ: **According as he hath chosen us in him** before the foundation of the world, that we should be holy and without blame before him **in love.**"* Notice the words that are in bold; we are already blessed with everything we that God has for us. We will not be getting more spiritual when we pass on to the other side. Paul confirms this by saying that we have everything now, which we had before the fall of humankind in Genesis 3. God does not want us to walk in His shadow, but in front of Him IN LOVE. This means that anything we send out into the world (actions, attitude, words, feelings, etc.) will hit God in the face! This is for our protection as well as all humanity. If we send out the wrong message, God has already forgiven His enemies and blessed those that have done Him wrong. It is now our turn to extend to others what He has given to us.

Jesus told his disciples, *"But I say unto you, Love your enemies, bless them that curse you, do good to them that hate you, and pray for them which despitefully use you, and persecute you; That ye may be the children of your Father which is in heaven: for he maketh his sun to rise on the evil and on the good, and sendeth rain on the just and on the unjust"*(Matthew 5:44-45).

Paul writes in Colossians 1:25-29, *"Whereof I am made a minister, according to the dispensation of God which is given to me for you,* **to fulfill the word of God; Even the mystery which hath been hid from ages and from generations, but NOW is made manifest to his saints:** *To whom God would make known what is the riches of the glory of this mystery among the Gentiles; which is Christ in you, the hope of glory: Whom we preach, warning every man, and teaching every man in* **all wisdom**; *that we may present* **every man** *perfect in Christ Jesus: Whereunto I also labor, striving according to his working, which worked in me mightily."*

Paul is not referring to "laboring" as something that still needs to be completed, but allowing the righteousness of God in him to be in control. God is not watching us sin while sitting on a throne somewhere in the sky. God is with us when we sin.

Truth is: the righteousness of God is mightily in each of us working as Christ. Our "faith" confession moves into "fact" acknowledgment depending on how complete and real we believe in Christ Jesus.

THE MYSTERY OF GOD IS:

- Christ is <u>in</u> all human vessels
- God sees every human perfect in Christ
- God is working mightily in each of us

As long as we are justifying behavior patterns, we are missing a true relationship with God. For us to see the manifestation of the revelation of who we already are we must rest in true son-ship with God that exalts, declares and reveals Him as Father to all humankind.

Questions about Bible verses…

1 Thessalonians 4:16

For the Lord himself (Christ in us) *shall descend* (come forth) *from* (our) *heaven* (our inner most being) *with a shout* (it is finished), *with the voice* (our mouth is His) *of the archangel* (messenger, us, God speaking from the beginning or who we were before the fall of Adam), *and with the trump of God* (priest would blow the Ram's horn to declare jubilee is now. Jesus is the Ram that died for us to have a horn to blow that it is finished), *and the dead* (those that are ignorant of truth) *in Christ* (of their true identity) *shall rise* (resurrection life will happen in a twinkle of the Holy Spirit unveiling revelation of their identity in Him) *first* (women /soul, and children /flesh are given covering first. These would be people that rest in the outer and middle courts with the Father. John writes about this is 1 John 2).

Verse 17:

Then we (first fruit, over comers, Elohim) *which are alive* (being the manifested sons of God) *remain* (continue being the manifested sons of God) *shall be caught up* (seized) *together with them* (those in the middle and outer court) *in the clouds* (witness of God identity) *to meet the Lord* (Elohim) *in the air* (unity of the body by the connection of our words speaking the character and nature of our true identity in Him. We manifest together the headship of Jesus Christ with the mind of Christ) *and so shall we ever* (it is finished) *be* (identity is in Him) *with the Lord* (mind of Christ).

God is all in ALL (1 Corinthians 15:28).

Christ is all in ALL (Ephesians 1:23).

The earth (all mankind) *belongs to the Lord and the fullness* (every person is a part of the body) *thereof.* (Jesus Christ said it was finished. The sacrifice was completed to cover the existence of ALL sin and separation. He now has a perfect bride. We that understand this (star company) are responsible for encouraging and ministering to the children (dust) and women (sand) seeing them through the eyes of God and believing it is finished and that all will come to know this by the drawing of the love of God they see in the first fruits.

1 John 3:2

Beloved (one that He has revealed Himself in intimacy to) *now* (today conception has taken place) *are we* (first fruit, star company) *the sons* (to do the Father's business) *of God* (when you see me you see the Father. The life I now live…Gal 2:20), *and it doth not yet appear what we shall be (*what member of the body); *but we know* (intimate, conception) *that, when he* (Christ in us) *shall appear* (light has a spectrum of many colors, yet each color is necessary for the fullness of Light. We don't know how or where we will be used to give birth to the body, but) *we shall be like Him* (there is only one body); *for we shall see him as he is* (when we are sitting in heavenly places, or the inner court with Christ, we are able to see through the veil of man's imagination that has kept us for a time in Pentecost or Passover understanding.)

God gives us the natural to understand the spiritual. When a couple come together in the bedroom in love; inner court, identity exchange through intimacy; conception takes place. The identity they went into the bedroom has been changed. That seed of life is carried back into the other rooms of the house. Those that may be in the other rooms may have walls of imagination and ego to where they do not initially connect to the "sweet spirit" of unconditional love that radiates from the couple that were in the bedroom. However, light removes darkness. The more those that know their identity as a son of God come into the presence of religion, doctrine, and ignorance with His presence and identity of Love, Life, and Light; there will be power and authority of the goodness of God drawing them to change into their true identity in Christ (Romans 2:4). Our life is not our own. We were bought with a price. When we receive revelation and understanding of who we are in Christ it is not for us to have an ego trip, but to go and multiply filling the earth with His glory, or more sons. God does not need children to have children, but those mature in Christ to do the Father's business of producing and raising children in love.

Notes of reflection and meditation

What were your immediate thoughts as you read this chapter?

_____

_____

_____

_____

_____

_____

What seemed confusing from what you thought?

_____

_____

_____

_____

_____

_____

What was something new that you had not heard before?

_____

_____

_____

_____

_____

_____

CHAPTER 12

Mystery of Iniquity

"And **now** *ye know what withholdeth that he might be revealed in his time. For the* **mystery of iniquity** *doth already work* (each person is going through their own battle with the flesh)*: only he who now letteth will let, until he* (*the* old Adam) *be taken out of the way. And then shall that Wicked be revealed* (ego), *whom the Lord shall consume* (take in) *with the spirit of his mouth* (the Word of God), *and shall destroy with the brightness* (truth) *of his coming* (out of our inner most being)*: Even him* (religion), *whose coming is after the working of Satan* (has the power and authority as a son of God, but uses the Word of God for self-ego) *with all power and signs and lying wonders, And with all deceivableness of unrighteousness in them that perish; because they received not the love* (unconditional) *of the truth, that they might* (already are) *be saved"* (2 Thessalonians 2:6-10).

Theologians to justify a coming antichrist have used these verses, but what Paul is really writing about is the **coming forth of Christ** in each of us. Calvary took away the iniquity of sin over 2000 years ago. We can find this in John 1:29, which read, *"Behold the Lamb of God, which taketh away THE SIN of the world."* Then in Luke 3:6, we read, *"ALL flesh shall see the SALVATION of God,"* not the wrath of an angry God, but the love of a Father that gave His own life for the children whom He created in His own image (John 3:16 and Genesis 1:26-27).

God is not mad at us when we miss the mark; however, mark missing will have consequences to the flesh and soul. God removed the offense of the mark (sin), but not the ability to miss the mark. Our mark missing ability does not offend God or change our established identity of being His son, but it does cause us a hindrance of having a relationship with God **out of our own condemnation and guilt**. We do not have the power to lose our identity in Him because the power of His grace is stronger. Again, our own guilt and condemnation hinder us from believing this truth.

The strength of sin is the law that causes guilt and condemnation. In the past, the church has been taught by theologians who have mixed grace with law keeping the church from entering **boldly** before the throne room of God where they would find His unconditional love, mercy and peace (Hebrews 4:16). How often have we heard Christians share "Jesus loves you just as you are, with all of your baggage? Just come and believe that He has died for your sin, confessing that you are a sinner, and then receive His grace for eternal life." Does this sound familiar? First, we are not a sinner. There has not been one since Calvary. Second, isn't it interesting that their doctrine teaches that Jesus receives us with all of our "baggage," but once we start going to church we receive condemnation and guilt if we still have the "baggage?"

How many people have changed trying to conform to the church's ideas and concepts of what a Christian is supposed to be like so that they can fit in, instead of what God says? How many times has the church used scripture to justify themselves instead of loving the unloved with His grace? We have all been in a position where we were trying to conform to those that we have given allegiance to behind the pulpit; instead of focusing on the love and grace of our Heavenly Father who gave us His Spirit to teach us all things so that when others would see us, they would see Father.

"Buried with him in baptism, wherein also ye are risen with him through the faith of the operation of God, who hath raised him from the dead. And you, being dead in your sins and the uncircumcision of your flesh, hath he quickened together with him, having forgiven you all trespasses; Blotting out the handwriting of ordinances that was against us, which was contrary to us, and took it out of the way, nailing it to his cross; And having spoiled principalities and powers, he made a shew of them openly, triumphing over them in it" (Colossians 2:12-15).

IN ALL OF OUR MARK MISSING, WE HAVE NOT OFFENDED OUR HEAVENLY FATHER.

Yes, we have planted bad seed that must be dealt with. Yes, we have offended and hurt other people because of our own pride, arrogance, and self-will, or ego that must be dealt with. However; despite all these things, nothing can separate us from the love of our Heavenly Father (Romans 8:35-39). We have never lost favor with DAD.

What the Lamb of God took away was the wrath and anger that DAD had. God does not have the ability today to be offended by anything we could do. If He did, then the cross would be nullified and Jesus would not have completed the job at Calvary. The assurance of our salvation would be a question that could not be answered.

God built into the laws of the universe "cause and effect" or "sowing and reaping." When we do what we want to do we reap the consequences of it. However, just because we make wrong choices and miss the mark does not separate us from the love of our Father who died and gave His life for us reestablishing our ability to enter boldly into His presence. What will hold us back is not God, but our own judgment and condemnation of cause and affect. This is what Paul wrote about in Romans Chapters 7 and 8.

Learning what to sow and what to reap can be found in God's teachings and instructions in the Old Testament. This is not about our Salvation, but after receiving Jesus as our Lord, how do we learn to live an abundant life in the earth.

We have the ability to make a mess of things, but we do not have the ability, even while in a mess, to make God mad at us. God took away the STRIFE. Calvary removed something in man and something in God. The veil has been removed for us to enter the throne room of mercy, love, and forgiveness; but it has also been removed when seated on the mercy seat with the Father looking out at the middle court, outer court, and the ends of the world. There is no veil going into the presence of God, and there is no veil separating God from His people.

God took everything we ever did and everything we will ever do in the future placing it on Jesus letting out the fullness of HIS wrath and anger against man subjecting it upon Himself (Isaiah 53:10-11). He then looked upon the suffering of what Jesus went through and was satisfied never to inflict judgment on humankind again (John 5:22).

The word SIN means "missing the mark." It is based on our actions and relationship with God as Father. It is not our identity. God is the creator of mankind and He created us in His image and likeness. Jesus Christ's death, burial, and resurrection did not remove our ability to miss the mark, which may hold lifetime consequences. When we come to Him and confess our missing the mark, (our sins) it is for OUR cleansing. Father is not upset with us, but we cannot change what we do not believe needs changing. The point of repentance is to become conscious of missing the mark: we were eating the fruit from the Tree of Knowledge of Good and Evil instead of the Tree of Life. Repentance allows us to yield ourselves to God for Him to pick us up and shake off the dust of doing things in our flesh, and encouraging us to keep our eyes focused on His Kingdom and His Righteousness. God's will is for us to live a life as His son BEING the Light of the world (Matt. 5:14); for as He is so are we in this world (1 John 4:17).

Notes of reflection and meditation

What were your immediate thoughts as you read this chapter?

_____

_____

_____

_____

_____

_____

What seemed confusing from what you thought?

_____

_____

_____

_____

_____

_____

What was something new that you had not heard before?

_____

_____

_____

_____

_____

_____

_____

CHAPTER 13

Siphoned from the Dregs

(This article focuses primarily on the religious "dregs," and religious Babylon. Of course there are other "dregs" which we must also be drawn away from if we are to become "poured out wine to the nations.")

"Moab has been at ease from his youth and he has SETTLED ON HIS LEES, and has not been emptied from vessel to vessel, neither has he gone into captivity: therefore his taste remained in him and his scent has not changed" (Jeremiah 48:11 NKJV).

In the process of winemaking, yeast is added to juice whereby the fermentation process begins by transforming the sugar in the juice into alcohol. During this process, the fermenting wine needs to be siphoned off from the sludge (or dead yeast) which settles at the bottom of the container. There is a continual process of siphoning and moving the wine from one container to another to separate it from the dead yeast. With each siphoning, the wine becomes clearer, clearer, closer, and closer to the product for which it was intended. In winemaker terms, the sludge of dead yeast is called "LEES." If the wine has been allowed to settle for too long on the lees without being siphoned off ... it is ruined.

In the verse from Jeremiah, Moab settling on his lees, is a reference to vinegar that is supposed to be turned into wine, but has settled too long on the lees. This describes the same spiritual state as "arresting at ease in Zion," and is a condition which thousands upon thousands of Christians are in today and don't even realize it.

Therefore... what are the "lees" in the church system today; the dregs from which we must be siphoned? Well ... lees are dead yeast. Jesus warned the disciples to beware of the yeast of the Pharisees, and that was speaking of the dead traditional teachings of religious men mostly; the old worn out sludge and carnal interpretation of the scriptures that had been passed on for many generations. The lees of today are certainly that, but might also include our indifference and neglect of holy things, our modernism and worldliness in our "church services," and the formality and rigid control of men in those services rather than the complete direction and guidance of the Holy Spirit.

Beloved, I am going to keep this very short so that you might ask the Lord if and how any of this might apply to you. Many of you are probably already aware that the Lord is even now separating between the great crowd of Sunday morning churchgoers and those who really are serious with God. Yes, God is siphoning off from the dregs of religion a remnant for Himself; a select company who are even now being drawn together by a work of the Spirit through the fires of testing, tribulation and suffering so that they might become poured out wine to the nations. In order to become poured out wine to the nations though, one must first be siphoned off from the religious dregs that can spoil the wine.

The Spirit revealed the same things that I am sharing with you today to the apostle John while he was on the Isle of Patmos. John described the call to "be siphoned off from the dregs of religion" as a voice crying, "Come out of her my people." Those who respond to that voice have an opportunity to become the poured out wine of blessing to the nations. Those who do not respond to that call but rather "settle on their lees" ... well, unfortunately, they are in danger of becoming what John described as "the wine of the wrath of her (the harlot's) fornication." That is not a wine of blessing folks; it is spiritual and religious poison. Most of the people of the earth (and even many Christians today) are drunk with the wine of the wrath of the harlot's fornication.

Notes of reflection and meditation

What were your immediate thoughts as you read this chapter?

_____

_____

_____

_____

_____

_____

What seemed confusing from what you thought?

_____

_____

_____

_____

_____

What was something new that you had not heard before?

_____

_____

_____

_____

_____

_____

CHAPTER 14

The Will of God

"Praise be to the God and Father of our Lord Jesus Christ, who has blessed us in the heavenly realms with every spiritual blessing in Christ. or he chose us in him before the creation of the world to be holy and blameless in his sight. In love he predestined us to be adopted as his sons through Jesus Christ, in accordance with his pleasure and will to the praise of his glorious grace, which he has freely given us in the One he loves. In him we have redemption through his blood, the forgiveness of sins, in accordance with the riches of God's grace that he lavished on us with all wisdom and understanding. And he made known to us the mystery of his will according to his good pleasure, which he purposed in Christ, to be put into effect when the times will have reached their fulfillment to bring all things in heaven and on earth together under one head, even Christ. In him we were also chosen, having been predestined according to the plan of him who works out everything in conformity with the purpose of his will, in order that we, who were the first to hope in Christ, might be for the praise of his glory. And you also were included in Christ when you heard the word of truth, the gospel

of your salvation. Having believed, you were marked in him with a seal, the promised Holy Spirit, who is a deposit guaranteeing our inheritance until the redemption of those who are God's possession-to the praise of his glory" (Ephesians 1:3-14 NIV).

The will of God was purposed in Himself before we were ever created. We do not have to make it happen. If God ordained something, He will cause it to succeed. Therefore, only God can make something come to past. The mystery of the will of God is not a mystery anymore because He made it known to us (vs. 9). God shares His intentions, His will, and His purpose with His sons.

Verse 10 has been used by theologians in the dispensation of the fullness of time as a blocking point in receiving all that Paul was sharing in reference to the will of God. God does not just show up when we say "any minute." He comes in His fullness. God does not work on our deadlines. We are all pregnant with God, but our third trimester time is different in each of us.

What is the will of God? To gather in ONE ALL THINGS IN CHRIST. The heart of God is unity, but it must be IN CHRIST (vs. 11). God, as the Lion of Judah, tore down the wall that separated heaven and earth becoming the sacrificial Lamb that declared peace between God and all humankind. Christ is the only true unity.

To make peace God tore down the wall of offense that separated us from the throne of God allowing us to receive His will of unconditional love, mercy, and forgiveness. When we receive what he has freely given to us, we then can love someone else with that same unconditional love.

How do we learn what the will of God is? Jesus and Paul taught from their Bible called the Tanak, or Old Testament.

We are predestined according to the purpose of Him to work out of His purpose; not ours. Predestination is not about arriving at a place that has already been established somewhere off in the sky with mansions and streets of gold; and just because God has predestined a place for us doesn't mean that we will arrive if we don't cooperate with God. We are predestined to be conformed in the image of His will; in the image of His son; to be Christ in the earth.

Predestined is not a secure location, but a predetermined one. God has made peace with each of us and reconciled us all. He is a peace with the whole world. The thought of this offends many because we are not at peace with one another. God is not threatened; it is we. God created government to deal with lawlessness. He gave us predestination, but within this, He also gave us the ability to make choices. We must stay on the road that gets us to that destination.

God gave us the Holy Spirit to teach and guide us through "unction's within" witnessing the will of God with our spirit to help us make right choices. God will not stop us from making wrong choices because we will never be free from sin until we realize we are free to sin and God still loves us. The strength of sin is the law. When sin holds us in bondage by fear of wrong choices then we are hindered in receiving the fullness of our Father's love.

The thought that God is going to bring wrath upon us can actually push us into sin because it keeps us in bondage of believing that we can never be good enough to please God. When we realize that God does not stop loving us, we do not have the guilt of separation from God, but now must deal with the consequences of our own actions. If we miss the mark, it does not change the destination, but the time it takes to arrive. The destination has already been established. It is the times and the journey that brings each of our unique experiences when we arrive.

During the times when Moses was leading the children of God in the wilderness, they circled the same places for forty years in search of the Promised Land. Have you ever asked, "Why didn't they get the message after crossing the same path and leaving the same animal and mankind "discharges" that they were not going in the right direction?" Yet, is this not what we do today with our many denominations teaching and preaching the same messages we have heard for years? Maybe it is because of the comfort of familiarity with what we already know putting off the promises of God for a someday happening instead of truly desiring to walk in the will of God.

> *"If you believed Moses, you would believe me, for he wrote about me."*
> **John 5:46**

To get where God wants us to go we cannot have landmarks, but be like Abraham looking for a city whose builder and maker is God. Joshua was born during the time of the wandering in the wilderness questioning what was outside the realm of going round and round to places that he had already traveled. The Lord is not trying to make us comfortable but give us a "Godly dis-ease." God works all things according to HIS own will and counsel, not according to our prayers. He does not move according to how much emotionalism or fasting we conjure up in praying, but are we praying by lining ourselves up with the purpose and counsel of His will?

If we have pressure and confusion to try to make something happen then it probably is not the will of God. The outcome may be His will, but the timing may not. The pressure should be on God. This does not mean there will not be opposition, especially from religion, but there should be a peace that goes beyond our understanding so that when the manifestation is brought forth, only God will be glorified. If there is an "I" in the decision, it probably is not His will or His timing.

God only takes counsel from His own purpose, which does not include desperation. He will make adjustments in our lives, even when we miss the mark and go in the opposite direction, to bring us into His purpose that He has predestined for us in the unity of Christ. In an instant, God will bring us back into His will. The religious system applies law and justification into the grace of God making a hardship to obtain His will. God only takes counsel from Himself. If we tell God that we are a thousand miles from His grace, God does not hear the thousand miles. He hears the heart desire to be in His will and instantly we are in a position with what He has already predestined. His Love, not fear of death or wrath of God draws us to the Father!

We do not have to make up the lost time of being a thousand miles out to come back a thousand miles to pick up where we should have turned. God will use where we are at and instantly place us where He wants us to be. When we turn to God, after walking in the wrong direction we are instantly in His presence where ALL things are possible.

Restoration is putting us back in the original or better than what we were. We began in Adam. He has restored us in Christ Jesus. We are not just the old Adam camouflaged as new, but today, we are completely and completely new in Christ. The old Adam is completely gone.

Sinners or non-believers are not the ones holding back the purposes of God. They have not said "yes" to God to affect the purpose. Religious systems have said "yes" to God, but they tell God how to do His will. The purpose and the will of God are brought out by the church, not the world. God loves

"And I will restore to you the years that the locust has eaten, the cankerworm, and the caterpillar, and the palmerworm, my great army which I sent among you" **Joel 2:25.**

the world and extends His love and mercy to ALL. He is not mad at anyone. To be the church, we must BE His identity in the flesh revealing His will. God says, "Love your enemies and those that despitefully use you," yet we think that God is going to bomb and destroy those that we think are His enemies. He cannot tell us to do something He cannot do Himself.

Religion challenges us to question, "What is in it for me if I come to know Jesus as my Lord and Savior?" The will of God is to seek out "what we can do for others unconditionally." God is not cutting anyone out of His will. We choose not to judicious our inheritance, which is found in the saints. We must join ourselves with the saints and bless them. True leadership is "leader's hip" connection. Find someone to help them make their dreams come true and our success will automatically happen. Put your life in someone else's pouring your life in them.

Our lives are an account for what is duplicated in someone else's life that edifies and glorifies God! Our purpose is not to change the world, but to seed the world with the unconditional grace, mercy, and love of God knowing Him as our Heavenly Father.

Missing the mark is "living outside our godly identity." True godliness is living in a state of forgiveness. *"I tell you the truth, whatever you bind on earth will be bound in heaven, and whatever you loose on earth will be loosed in heaven"* (Matthew 18:18 NIV). It is the authority and opinions, which people express with their mouth that brings judgment and condemnation to others. If we would only stop and think before we speak recalling what Scripture tells us about judging others: *"Do not judge, or you too will be judged. **For in the same way you judge others, you will be judged,** and with the measure you use, it will be measured to you"* (Matthew 7:1-2 NIV).

It is not God who is judging humankind today. He did that over 2000 years ago when Jesus went to Calvary. Today, God judges no man

(John 5:22). This was given to us through John when Jesus walked the earth and it still exists today. *"For I am the LORD, I change not;"* (Mal. 3:6).

We do not have the power to reject the will of God anymore than we could stop our natural body from going through natural development. We can have a body of a teenager with a mind of a five year old; however, even in our natural understanding we acknowledge that this is not as it should be. The will of God is for us to grow up in Christ to be the manifestation of His sons so that when others see the son they see their Father. By the love of the Father the son releases to the world, those that know not God as their Father are drawn to Him by His love that is manifested through the son.

"The Spirit itself beareth witness with our spirit, that we are the children of God: And if children, then heirs; heirs of God, and joint-heirs with Christ; if so be that we suffer with him, that we may be also glorified together. For I reckon that the sufferings of this present time are not worthy to be compared with the glory which shall be revealed in us. For the earnest expectation of the creature waiteth for the manifestation of the sons of God" (Romans 8:16-19).

Notes of reflection and meditation

What were your immediate thoughts as you read this chapter?

_____

_____

_____

_____

_____

_____

What seemed confusing from what you thought?

_____

_____

_____

_____

_____

_____

What was something new that you had not heard before?

_____

_____

_____

_____

_____

_____

_____

CHAPTER 15

In Search of the Fathers' of the Faith

"Behold, I will send you Elijah the prophet before the coming of the great and dreadful day of the Lord: And he shall turn the heart of the fathers' to the children, and the heart of the children to their fathers, lest I come and smite the earth with a curse." (Malachi 4:5-6)

These verses are the last two verses found in the Old Testament of the Bible. Between the Old and New Testament there was approximately a 400 year span that the voice of the Lord was not heard through any prophets. This prophetic word from Malachi comes during a time period after the temple in Jerusalem had been completed. Abuse had come into the sacrificial system of the priesthood, and the overall spiritual state of the people was in decline. Divorce was widespread (Malachi 2:14), mixed marriages were being contracted (Malachi 2:10-12), there were offerings of blemished sacrifices (Malachi 1:6-14), and people failing to pay tithes (Malachi 3:8-10), were all part of the life style during these times. Many theologians believe that God was silent during these 400 years allowing mankind to take charge of his own self destruction.

After this prophecy was given to the people of God, it became a custom while celebrating the Feast of Pentecost, for the Jewish people to place an empty chair at their table with a glass of wine in anticipation that Elijah would return. When the spirit of Elijah returned, the people would anticipate the fulfillment of this prophetic word. They would eagerly look for the return of fathers' to their children and children to their fathers so that the earth would not be cursed. Centuries of restoration have been taking place, yet even today, the Jewish people are still looking for Elijah. They believe that this will be the sign of knowing that the Messiah's coming is near, and then, there will be peace on earth.

As I was doing research on this topic I found it interesting that the name "Malachi" means "messenger of the Lord." Following the end of the Old Testament we begin with the book of Matthew. His name means "gift of Jehovah." Matthew begins where Malachi left off four hundred years later, with fathers having sons from Abraham to Jesus Christ.

Many people skip over the first chapter of Matthew because it seems boring with just a generational history lesson. What appeals to me is that the four hundred years that theologians consider God to be silent, He is actually putting the fine tuning into manifestation of the coming of the Lord. Each of the fathers in Matthew Chapter One is recognized because they produced (begat) a son. Whether or not they were recognized for anything else in history, the one thing they did which was of great significance is to keep the lineage from Abraham going of a father to a son, and then a son becoming a father to produce a son until the birth of Jesus Christ. This tells me that God was very busy when others thought He was silent. He was putting the fine touches of completion to the salvation of mankind. Each father had to have an understanding of the vision and significance of the Abraham covenant to keep the desire to father a son; and each son had to have a relationship with their father to want to inherit that vision to give to their own son as expressed in Malachi 4:5-6. This is a heart's desire that comes from knowing God and believing God by faith as Abraham did.

Today, God speaks to us by His Son, Jesus Christ, through the power of the Holy Spirit versus the prophets. The difference between a Son and a child of God is a Son must mature into the position of doing the Father's business. His passion and heart cry must be to glorify His Father, and not himself, so that all that he says and does will be to draw others to the Father. As Sons, we are to be the expressed image of God's glory, His person. We are the touchable of the Father's image to the world. Do people hear the voice of their Heavenly Father calling them by name in love into a closer relationship with Him through our hearts and mouths? Do others see unconditional love, forgiveness, and peace when we speak; or do they hear Scripture quoted bringing justification and condemnation?

We are the touchable, tangible image of God who is Spirit for the world to see.

In I Corinthians 4:14-16, Paul considers it his responsibility of being a father to the Corinthians by referring to them as his sons. He does not desire to shame them, but to warn them of the direction they were taking in their Christian walk. What is interesting is that he points out that there are ten-thousand instructors in Christ, but not many fathers among them. If we apply this today we could say we have lots of men and women on the platform in our churches, but how many of them would be considered as fathers? Please keep in mind that in scripture, the term father is a spiritual identity of maturity in the natural, just as the word son is. We are given natural fathers as a type and shadow for understanding spiritual implication, but God is both male and female according to Genesis 1:27.

So what kind of person is this "spiritual father" that Paul refers to? In the natural, a father is one that has raised his children, passing on his genes, and the goodness of his identity. The children recognize their identity as the father's sons because of his name which carries honor and authority. The father does not look for glory and recognition, but knows that when his children come to a point in their lives where they talk and do their business as he did, then his own glory will come. Fathers get taken advantage of when their children are still children. There is no honor to a father to see his grown children still living as a dependent child not able to handle his own affairs. However, when a father sees his children working through their lives in the way they were taught by their parents, there is great joy to the parents.

Anyone can come and mesmerize a congregation with revelation knowledge from the Lord that will impregnate their spirit. However, Paul tells us in I Corinthians 4:15 that very few teachers are there to nurture the birth of this revelation allowing the spirit to grow and develop. This leaves a child with spiritual power, but no one to help them grow in wisdom, and know how to give glory to the Father. Galatians 4:1-2 tells us that it takes the heart of a father's love and wisdom to help the child grow up with understanding of Son-ship of our Heavenly Father. Many times we are asked, "What would Jesus do?", but few of us really allow the son-ship of Jesus Christ to flow through our minds and bodies because we are not taught how to be sons. Jesus did not consider it robbery to be equal with God, yet very few churches will acknowledge that this should be our mind as believers of His body. Instead, we are as children searching for our identity of where we fit. We know who Jesus is, but we are not able to consider our true identity as His brother/sister in Christ, and the power and responsibility of that position.

Individuals with a calling to be an evangelist, teacher, prophet, apostle, or pastor are supposed to walk in their gifting with the heart of a father. However, many of them share wonderful Biblical wisdom on a platform, and then disappear in a crowd. The church was given the five-fold ministry as the hand of God to be "fathers" to the children. How many of these "fathers" are staying home raising their children versus coming to preach on Sunday mornings, stirring the children up with a good time party, and then taking off when a bigger and better opportunity arises? A father has a responsibility to seek out the children: watching, praying, staying awake late at night with concern about EACH one, letting none of his children lack or suffer in any way that he has been given responsibility for. He knows with an intimacy of knowing, and loves with a passion that cuts to his heart for each of the members of his congregation. He worries when the children are rebellious wanting to go in a different direction that is not like Jesus.

Jesus illustrated this for us when he prays to the Father in John Chapter 17. This prayer tells us that Jesus knew his responsibility was to show the disciples the Father through himself. He made sure that his work was completed and none of the disciples were lost that the Father gave him to minister to.

The church is a family affair. Father's should be "hovering" over the children of God to protect and discipline them in love rather than "ruling" them with judgment and condemnation. Paul told the Corinthians in I Corinthians 4:15 that he fathered them through the gospel; that his ways are in Christ, which is what he taught everywhere, in every church. They were manifesting the gifts of the Spirit of God, but they were not reflecting the heart of the Father which is why Paul was correcting them. Paul was not withdrawing the significance of the gifts, but without love, they were just showing off and glorifying themselves. This is what we see even today in much of the church and the gifting God has given to the body.

Churches today lack the supernatural power of God because they have not kept the pattern of father and son relationship in Jesus Christ. When others see a Christian they should be seeing Jesus, and in turn be drawn unto their Heavenly Father. Jesus showed us that the life of God is manifested at the midnight hours of our lives where there is no yesterday and tomorrow isn't here yet. It is a moment of eternity in the midst of time that comes forth. If you go to your past to search for answers then you are out of covenant, and if you move forward with your own thoughts and ideas you are out of covenant. It can only be Jesus, not Jesus "plus" our own way. It is at this moment, that the supernatural power of God is manifested in the Sons of God.

In Matthew 16:15-18, Jesus asked the disciples who they thought he was after they had just discussed that the people considered Him to be either John the Baptist, Elijah, Jeremiah, or one of the other prophets. Peter spoke up and said, "Thou art the Christ, the Son of the living God." Jesus responds to this revelation that Peter received saying that it came from the Father of Jesus, and it is with this wisdom that JESUS will build His church, not man. Jesus shares in John 20:17 that his Father is our Father, and his God is our God. Jesus keeps the father and son covenant continuing with the lineage of Abraham by telling us that as the Father sent him, he sends us (John 20:21). This type of relationship crosses over from Old Testament to New Testament showing us that God is eternal and not limited to time. It was by faith that Abraham rested believing God that his seed would bless all the nations of the earth (Genesis 22:18).

God came to Abraham to initiate His ways beginning in Genesis Chapters 12-22. If the fathers/leaders (the five-fold ministry covering of your church) are not in Christ, following after Jesus to build the church, then you won't see Christ. When people say, "I am a servant of the most High God", or "I am a sinner saved by grace", yet they have been a believer for a season in the body of Christ, they may sound religious, but in reality they are still children and not mature as Sons. They are not edifying the Father and building up the body of Christ with His power and authority, but are using their own ability in works to keep the body of Christ together. They are staying focused on themselves in a religious way versus moving forward to maturing and bringing the reflection of Jesus Christ for the world to see. Instead, they reflect immature behaviors of self-centeredness, rebellion, hurt feelings, pride, discomfort, and are easily offended. They are as children without power, authority, or influence lacking the ability to manifest the supernatural power of the Father (Galatians 4:1-2).

The kingdom of God is as the smallest seed becoming the largest tree. Abraham's faithfulness is what has kept the promise. Scripture shows us that each generation has a double portion of inheritance as illustrated by Elijah giving his mantel to Elisha because he stood with his father (2 Kings). The spirit of Elijah spoken of in Malachi represents kingdom order of a Father and son relationship. This prophecy was fulfilled with John the Baptist according to Luke 1:17. What will save the earth from a curse is getting the earth in proper alignment. God is after the father's heart to turn it toward the children, and then the children's hearts will be turned to the Father. When we go through life trying to possess the land our way, we have a mindset of telling God how to be God. God will not bless our mess. The most destructive answer we can get from God in answer to our prayers is for Him to say nothing, but allow us to continue in our own self destruction until we realize it is ALL God, and only God in ALL.

As Christians, we pray asking God to bless our confusion, but we are not willing to align ourselves up to the order of God for the blessing to flow. We play a game of hit and miss with God by dying to ourselves for a moment, and then after He has taken over the situation, we raise up the old man to live with the new, and wonder why God isn't answering prayers. We then try to justify our natural understanding by saying, "maybe it is not God's will for me not to be healed, or maybe He wants me to go through this because I must suffer first before being blessed." We justify the circumstance by what we see versus walking in faith of what we should believe Scripture tells us. We also look at things from the level of a child or at the foot of the cross, rather than the position of Son- ship which is resurrection power from death, hell, and the grave.

John the Baptist was the son doing the Father's business declaring for all to "prepare ye the way." His life was an illustration of how "the way" is prepared with his own head being cut off. This

Is there a dead man, the old Adam talking to you between your ears?

is a type and shadow to teach us that we are to have the mind of Christ by beheading ourselves as believers, and being crucified with Christ (Galatians 2:20). The life we now live in the flesh is Christ by the faith of the Son of God. We are to take on the mind of Christ, and not our natural understanding. This mind is the key to our inheritance of aligning our spirit, soul, and body with His. We must protect this inheritance by the words of our mouth and the mind set of our heart anxiously desiring to develop this inheritance, to pass it on with a double portion of blessing to our children. The inheritance of the Sons of God is not the cross, but the resurrection (Galatians 2:21-3:3, 13).

Jesus is the firstborn to bring the pattern of the old into redeeming the world. He is not just a savior or redeemer. He is the FIRST BEGOTTEN SON of GOD. He gave us the covenant of a Son. Being a child of God does not give a believer automatic access into the inheritance of God. Everyone is given the power to become Sons of God, but not everyone succeeds (John 1:12). A Son of God is revealed by the power of God being manifested in love, not personal edification. Signs and wonders follow behind Sons of God (Acts 5:15). Children are looking for them (John 4:48), and then running to and fro trying to possess them (Daniel 12:4).

In Genesis Chapter 9, we read about the story of Noah and his sons after the flood. Life is starting over for his family. They plant a vineyard; made up some wine; and then Noah indulges a little too much, and is found drunk and naked by his son Canaan. Did you ever wonder why, when Noah finds out that Canaan went and told his brothers about what he saw, that Noah cursed him, but blessed the other two sons? It wasn't that Noah loved the other two sons more than Canaan, but that Canaan was just as much a son as his brothers, yet he refused to grow-up, and therefore would be a servant versus a son. When Canaan saw his father drunk and naked the first thing he did was to play the childish game of telling a secret. He disgraced his father versus standing in the gap as a covering. Once the other brothers became aware of the situation, they took covering on their shoulders and walked backwards so they didn't see their father's nakedness, and then they covered him. The shoulders represent authority. Shem and Japheth were not making judgment on Noah by walking backwards, but acting as a shield of son-ship to protect their father from anything while he was in a vulnerable state.

The church of Jesus Christ is to be built where the gates of hell cannot prevail against it. Satan should not be allowed in the house of God for there is no place for the devil (Ephesians 4:27). Yet, he is welcomed in through the doors of: gossip, complacency, denominational doctrines, theology, religious rituals, and self-centered Christianity. Churches today do not align themselves with the son-ship of Jesus Christ which is why there is no power. There is an abundance of sickness, disease, poverty, depression, divorce, etc. inside most churches. Many times when people have exposed their personal struggles, conflicts, and sins for prayer request, this information becomes passed on as gossip in the name of needing prayer. A true Son of God would take what has been shared, lift it up to the Father, and declare by the power and authority of the name of Jesus that it is a finished work (healed, completed, satisfied, restored) according to John 19:30. Most people are still in a vulnerable state, and therefore it is up to the Son that received the prayer request to also be the intercessor, as a hedge of protection to believe by faith, that the issues are a finished work until the full manifestation is seen. The church should be setting an example for the world as a place of healing, wholeness, life, love, and peace. When a person comes into a place where the Sons of God are present, there should be a distinguishing presence of heaven on earth.

It took thirty years for Jesus to grow and develop into the understanding of his true identity as the Son of God, and his purpose on this earth. In Luke 3:21-22, we are told that heaven was opened when Jesus was baptized in the Jordan River. When a person is baptized, it means that the person you were a few seconds before going into the water, and who you are coming out of the water after being immersed, are two different people. The Jordan River represents death of the old man. When Jesus came up from being baptized a voice came from heaven saying, "Thou art my beloved Son; in thee I am well pleased" (verse 21). From that moment on, Jesus had a responsibility to be about the Father's business so that when others saw Him, they saw the Father. Before the Jordan he was living a life as the child of Mary and Joseph, but after his baptism His whole focus was to reflect his identity as the Son of God.

Today, we have many children of God refusing to grow up. They believe that if they have received Jesus as their personal savior, they go to church, read their Bible, and try to be a good person for their family and community, that they consider themselves to be are mature Christians. This is not the Biblical definition of being mature in Christ.

A mature Christian is one that has the confidence and wisdom of our Heavenly Father to know His power and authority, and apply it to everyday life situations. They walk by faith, not by sight knowing that their Father judges no man (John 5:22), and that His mercy endures forever (Psalm 136). They look unto Jesus (to see the Father) to learn how to respond to the world issues, to pray, and to seek wisdom of unconditional love, mercy, and forgiveness without bringing attention to self. They believe that it is their Father's will that none shall perish (2 Peter 3:9), and that they have a responsibility to stand in the gap of intercession for the lost sheep until ALL one-hundred percent have come back to the Father. The body of Christ cannot be blemish-free without ALL of the "lost Adam linage" being returned to the Father.

Where do you fit in with the growth and development of being a Christ One? Are you about doing the Father's business, or are you looking out for yourself, being a good Christian and waiting to get to heaven someday?

"Finally, be ye all of one mind, having compassion one of another, love as brethren, be pitiful, be courteous: note rendering evil for evil" (I Peter 3:8-9a). Peter tells us that we are all to have one mind, the mind of Jesus Christ. As the bride of Christ, we are a corporate body. If one person is lost, whether in the flesh, or out of the flesh, the body of Christ cannot be complete until we intercede to bring them out of hell or darkness. Jesus didn't send them there; we did with our thoughts and words by believing in tradition and denominational religion instead of allowing Jesus to build His church.

If we truly have a heart's desire to see the return of Jesus, we must be willing to change allowing the Sons of God to come forth bringing unity and wholeness to His body. May this teaching bless you with the Father's love and your true identity in Christ Jesus.

Notes of reflection and meditation

What were your immediate thoughts as you read this chapter?

_____

_____

_____

_____

_____

_____

What seemed confusing from what you thought?

_____

_____

_____

_____

_____

_____

What was something new that you had not heard before?

_____

_____

_____

_____

_____

_____

Father's Love Letter

By Bryan Adams

My Child...
You may not know me, but I know everything about you...Psalm 139:1
I know when you sit down and when you rise up...Psalm 139:2
I am familiar with all your ways...Psalm 139:3
Even the very hairs on your head are numbered...Matthew 10:29-31
For you were made in my image...Genesis 1:27
In me you live and move and have your being...Acts 17:28
For you are my offspring...Acts 17:28
I knew you even before you were conceived...Jeremiah 1:4-5
I chose you when I planned creation...Ephesians 1:11-12
You were not a mistake, for all your days are written in my book...Psalm 139:15-16I determined the exact time of your birth and where you would live...Acts 17:26
You are fearfully and wonderfully made...Psalm 139:14
I knit you together in your mother's womb...Psalm 139:13
And brought you forth on the day you were born...Psalm 71:6
I have been misrepresented by those who don't know me...John 8:41-44
I am not distant and angry, but am the complete expression of love...1 John 4:16
And it is my desire to lavish my love on you...1 John 3:1
Simply because you are my child and I am your father...1 John 3:1
I offer you more than your earthly father ever could...Matthew 7:11
For I am the perfect father...Matthew 5:48
Every good gift that you receive comes from my hand...James 1:17
For I am your provider and I meet all your needs...Matthew 6:31-33
My plan for your future has always been filled with hope...Jeremiah 29:11
Because I love you with an everlasting love...Jeremiah 31:3
My thoughts toward you are countless as the sand on the seashore...Psalm 139:17-18
And I rejoice over you with singing...Zephaniah 3:17
I will never stop doing good to you...Jeremiah 32:40
For you are my treasured possession...Exodus 19:5
I desire to establish you with all my heart and all my soul...Jeremiah 32:41
And I want to show you great and marvelous things...Jeremiah 33:3
If you seek me with all your heart, you will find me...Deuteronomy 4:29

Delight in me and I will give you the desires of your heart...Psalm 37:4
For it is I who gave you those desires...Philippians 2:13
I am able to do more for you than you could possibly imagine...
    Ephesians 3:20
For I am your greatest encourager...2 Thessalonians 2:16-17
I am also the Father who comforts you in all your troubles...
    2 Corinthians 1:3-4
When you are brokenhearted, I am close to you...Psalm 34:18
As a shepherd carries a lamb, I have carried you close to my heart...Isaiah
    40:11
One day I will wipe away every tear from your eyes...Revelation 21:3-4
And I'll take away all the pain you have suffered on this earth...
    Revelation 21:3-4
I am your Father, and I love you even as I love my son, Jesus...John 17:23
For in Jesus, my love for you is revealed...John 17:26
He is the exact representation of my being...Hebrews 1:3
He came to demonstrate that I am for you, not against you...Romans 8:31
And to tell you that I am not counting your sins...2 Corinthians 5:18-19
Jesus died so that you and I could be reconciled...2 Corinthians 5:18-19
His death was the ultimate expression of my love for you...1 John 4:10
I gave up everything I loved that I might gain your love...Romans 8:31-32
If you receive the gift of my son Jesus, you receive me...1 John 2:23
And nothing will ever separate you from my love again...Romans 8:38-39
Come home and I'll throw the biggest party heaven has ever seen...
    Luke 15:7
I have always been Father, and will always be Father...Ephesians 3:14-15
My question is...Will you be my child?...John 1:12-13
I am waiting for you...Luke 15:11-32

Love,
Your Dad, Almighty God

*(Father's Love Letter used by permission Father Heart Communications © 1999 www.
FathersLoveLetter.com)*

$\mathcal{L}ife$ $\mathcal{L}essons$ $from$
$\mathcal{T}he$ $\mathcal{B}ook$ of $\mathcal{N}ehemiah$

The Old Testament was not written for the purpose of providing history lessons; but to give instructions, illustrations, definitions, and types/shadows for us to see God's plan in bringing forth the sons of God on the earth. It shows us the way to walk and also how not to walk. God uses the Old Testament to express truths that are present today for with God there is no past tense. What the children of Israel walked through in the Old Testament is still being walked out by the church today.

Jerusalem signifies the house of God, the city of God. It is a city surrounded by a wall with gates. Today we hear of the "golden gates" which will surround Jerusalem when the Lord returns. This is a city that has gone through destruction and rebuilding more than any other city around the world. However, the wall that God is building today is not a part of the literal city of Jerusalem, but the people, or church. We are the temple of God today (I Corinthians 3:17).

God is bringing forth a remnant of people around the world today to declare His city. In these scriptures this is represented by the people that have escaped the bondage of Babylon. They were free but had lost the foundation and understanding required to have a relationship with God. Religious confusion had replaced relationship.

The first concern that Nehemiah had was to rebuild the walls of Jerusalem. Those that had returned to Jerusalem had no way to defend themselves. Rebuilding these walls was accomplished over a 25 year period, which took place about 400 years before Christ. It didn't just happen within a few years, but was a vision that was diligently pursued for a long time with many people having to put aside their own issues of fatigue. They didn't have the miracles of Jesus or the letters of Paul to encourage them. It was the faith and vision God gave Nehemiah that allowed them to persevere.

Today, there is a loud trumpet call being given to rebuild the walls of Zion. The vision that Nehemiah was given to rebuild the wall of the city of God had been a trumpet call as well. This is the same trumpet that is heard in the book of Revelation to return and establish the foundational walls of Christianity.

Nehemiah faced a tremendous amount of hardship in taking on this project. His workmen had to defend themselves from their enemies while they were trying to work to rebuild the wall. They were continually ridiculed with words that demeaned their craftsmanship being told by outsiders that what they were doing would not stand the test of time, and that their work was irrelevant to the city of God. This was a very long, tedious project that was draining on the people emotionally, physically, and spiritually. Theologically, building this wall compares to us today building our own wall so that deception of religious bondage cannot penetrate the revelation of LIFE that the Holy Spirit has revealed to us.

There were military attacks which tried to deter the children of God from building this wall. This book illustrates the persistent will that took place when God placed a vision in the heart of those that He had called. The wall was intended to secure the city so that it would be possible to inhabit the Holy City again. For us today, our "Holy City" is being in the presence of God and knowing the UNCONDITIONAL love that He has for us as Father despite the opposition where scriptures are used to bring condemnation and justification.

Nehemiah's vision was not only the preparation of the walls to inhabit the city safely, but to bring restoration to the temple on Mount Zion. The other concern he had was the recovery of the Law of Moses, and the faithful interpretation and observation of the sacred word. The vision the Lord gave him was not only to protect the city, but to have the truth of the word of God be restored in the city.

Nehemiah was a builder and an administrator. The Scribe Ezra, who lived during this time, was given the responsibility by Nehemiah to re-establish the Law of the Covenant. Ezra had spent his whole life copying and studying the law. He knew it better than any other person that lived. They were concerned about the proper interpretation of the law that had gone astray during exile.

Hundreds of years before this time when God's people were in the wilderness with Moses, there was only a remnant that crossed over into the Promised Land even though the word of the Lord had been given to them. What God gave them was more than the laws of Moses. It included the Law of the Covenant that all the children of Israel had received. Yet, while in the wilderness sin and contamination entered into their lives. Just like Moses and Joshua, Nehemiah and Ezra came to renew the Covenant of God with the people. They desired to bind the people to God on the basis of the Word, and reestablish Truth.

The people had been without the wisdom and knowledge of what God originally established among His people for such a long time that it was necessary for them to go back to the foundation to re-establish the Law of the Covenant. Ezra took on the responsibility to establish the law in the hearts of the people keeping out sin and disobedience. He called the assembly together as Moses did to establish the Covenant by reading the words likened to a trumpet sound. He then sprinkled the blood of sacrifice upon the altar first, and then upon the people, binding them together in covenant unto God.

We begin with the Book of Nehemiah, Chapter One, using the Amplified Bible:

With verse 3 - 11 we read that Nehemiah was given a message about what is taking place in Jerusalem with the people of God. When he heard that the people were in great affliction and reproach, it stirred his heart to the point that he wept taking upon himself to pray, fast, and plead before God for the people's situation. He then began to intercede for the people reminding God of His words to Moses:

Verse 8-9: *"Remember (earnestly) what You commanded Your servant Moses: If you transgress and are unfaithful, I will scatter you abroad among the nations; but if you return to Me and keep My commandments and do them, though your outcasts were in the farthest part of the heavens (the expanse of outer space), yet will I gather them from there and will bring them to the place in which I have chosen to set My Name."*

Nehemiah came to Jerusalem to restore the city with rebuilding the wall. The word "wall" means to join and protect. The wall that God is rebuilding today is not a physical place called Jerusalem, but people. However, these people must show the rebuilding of His temple as a type/shadow of the real. God is not going to permit the rebuilding while we just sit and wait for the Lord's return. He is making sure that there will be those that He has called to personally qualify for what only God will do. This book is full of specifics about the people that God chose to build what portion of what gate and what location of the wall. A whole teaching could be done about each person's name that is listed in this book declaring something unique and specific in the way God built the wall and re-established the city.

A wall represents the standard and boundaries of a city. It is the protection, limitation, and expression of a city. Today, Christ is living within a people. We are the temple of God. His coming forth will not be from the sky, but from within His temple. If we miss the coming of Christ it is because we were not looking in the temple of God, but somewhere else. Christ IN YOU is the hope of glory (Col. 1:27).

The golden gate that theologians have taught would be opened in Jerusalem when the Lord returns is a type and shadow for us to look within ourselves for a gate to be opened and the manifestation of Christ in us to be released. The Book of Nehemiah gives us a pattern to follow in the opening of this gate within the heart of each of us.

The wall that Nehemiah is called by God to build is a standard being set within a company of people that have been pulled aside by God to establish for His kingdom. However, whether we speak of the wall in Japan or in Jerusalem, they both make a specific statement to the world which is: This is the city and here is the expression of it. Here are the gates and entrance to enter into it and here is the place of exit. The walls state that within them there is protection and unity of like mind.

Nehemiah groans for the city and seeks the Lord for the repairing of it including the walls that protect it. The overwhelming task set before him is a project that he knows must be accomplished, but he also must depend on God for the resources and manpower to make it happen. He had served under a heathen king, but God touched the heart of Artaxerxes so that he was willing to supply Nehemiah with the means to rebuild Jerusalem.

Chapter 2:

Nehemiah begins to encourage the people showing the king's letter which gained access to supplies to rebuild the wall. In verse 11 we see that he was in Jerusalem for three days which spiritually speaks of resurrection, or a new beginning.

He then got up in the night after everyone else was asleep taking just a few men with him and an animal to ride on. What Nehemiah did not do is to go about telling a lot of people what God had put in his heart trying to get a committee or church group's approval.

He went out by the Valley Gate toward the Dragon's Well and to the dung Gate inspecting the gates that had been destroyed by fire. He then went to the Fountain Gate and to the King's Pool, but couldn't pass because the destruction was so great. So he rode by the brook (Kidron) in the night inspecting the wall, and then returned to the Valley Gate (13-15).

Verse 16 tells us that no one knew what Nehemiah was doing including the rulers, Jews, priests, nobles, officials, or even the people that did the work. God gave him a secret work to survey the situation and destruction that exists. No one had a clue that he was making an observation of the situation for God.

When Nehemiah has a good understanding of what the circumstance is with the city of Jerusalem and the wall that has been torn apart, he presents the situation to the people. In verse 18 we read, "Then I told them of the hand of my God which was upon me for good, and also the words that the king had spoken to me. And they said, Let us rise up and build! So they strengthened their hands for the good work."

Whenever God is doing a good work through us we can expect opposition of some kind. The same thing occurred for Nehemiah and the people that were supporting him to rebuild the wall. In verse 19 Nehemiah and the people were mocked with the words of Sanballat the Horonite, Tobiah an Ammonite servant, and Geshem who were Arab. They laughed, scorned, and despised Nehemiah and the people by saying "What is this thing you are doing? Will you rebel against the king?"

They didn't just express their opposition once and then walk away. We read in Chapter 4, verses 1 and 2, "But when Sanballat heard that we were building the wall, he was angry and in a great rage, and he ridiculed the Jews. And he said before his brethren and the army of Samaria, What are these feeble Jews doing? Will they restore things (at will and by themselves)? Will they (try to bribe their God) with sacrifices? Will they finish up in a day? Will they revive the stones out of the heaps of rubbish, seeing they are burned?"

Since his mockery didn't do anything against Nehemiah, Sanballat gathered the strength of the Samaritan army. Samaritans represent Jews that did not want to summit to the ways of God. They set up their own standard instead of God's.

Nehemiah is receiving the opposition of all those that are against what God has shown him. There is parallel with the Jews and Samaritans for us today. For example, we can see all the many Christian denominations that refuse to work together as one body, yet insist that their doctrine is the path to life according to the word of God. Nehemiah is going against all ridicule and enemy forces to do what God has shown him.

These people that worked on the rebuilding did not turn their backs to the enemy. While they worked, they carried swords and shields to fight off any attacks (vs. 17). They had to continually keep themselves protected as they were rebuilding. Keep in mind; this was not a 6 months or one year project, but took place over a 25 year period.

Many people died of old age before seeing the finished work, yet by faith they persevered.

With all the opposition around Nehemiah and the men that were rebuilding they prayed to God and set a watch against their enemies day and night. Those carrying the most burdens began to weaken, so Nehemiah set armed men behind the wall in places that were least protected. He used the people as families with their swords, spears, and bows.

In verse 4 of Chapter 4 we read, "(And Nehemiah prayed) *Hear, O our God, for we are despised. Turn their taunts upon their own heads, and give them for a prey in a land of their captivity.*"

The parallel that we see happening is what we go through today: God will be calling us out to do something that may not agree with church doctrine. We must pray about it waiting for His counsel while searching His word. Once we know in our heart without any question what God is commissioning, we must put on the armor of God expecting to be attacked with words of ridicule that will try and convince us that we are not really hearing from God.

The voice of the enemy will say things such as, "If God is in this: why hasn't He told everyone else; why is there so much financial struggle; why is it difficult to get the supplies that are needed; why are you and a few people the only ones hearing; why is there so much confusion; why are things going backwards after taking a few steps forward; why is there delay?"

These questions are not meant to be answered, but to weaken the vision and call of God. Therefore, it is vitally important to be equipped with the armor of God (Ephesians 6:13-18) expecting confrontation while moving towards what God has called us to do for His glory and His kingdom to be manifested NOW.

Nehemiah 4: 13-14, *"So I set (armed men) behind the wall in places where it was least protected; I even thus used the people as families with their swords, spears, and bows. I looked (them over) and rose up and said to the nobles and officials and the other people, Do not be afraid of the enemy; (earnestly) remember the Lord and imprint Him (on your minds), great and terrible, and (take from Him courage to) fight for your brethren, your sons, your daughters, your wives, and your homes."*

Further down in this chapter we read that the destruction of the wall was great and spread out. The workers were individually armed, but because of the distance between workers, they were to press on in diligence to the cause and vision God had given them independently.

This issue is addressed by Nehemiah in verses 19-21:

"And I said to the nobles and officials and the rest of the people, the work is great and scattered, and we are separated on the wall, one far from another; in whatever place you hear the sound of the trumpet, rally to us there. Our God will fight for us. So we labored at the work while half of them held the spears from dawn until the stars came out."

When God calls us to do something He equips us individually in accordance to the vessel that we are created for that purpose. Though it will be the same equipment, it may fit a little different on each person because we are all a unique portion of the body of Christ. However, once the trumpet sound is heard within our spirit (vs. 18), we will come together as His body for the same call that God has placed in each of our hearts.

In Chapter 5, the people began to complain about their debit and what it is costing them to build this wall. The kingdom of God requires a certain standard of excellence. God is not looking for a people that are interested in doing a "patch job" for His Kingdom to be manifested. He does not need a "buddy" to give Him an opinion of what works and doesn't work. Christ is all and in all (Col. 3:11). It takes those that know they are a new creature in Christ (Gal. 6:15) ready to do the Father's business. They believe in their heart that as He is so am I in this world (I John 4:17). The old man (Adam) is gone and all things are new in Him (2 Corinth. 5:17). God requires perfection from those that He has called.

The people's complaints to Nehemiah were about a burden they were carrying as a debit or bondage that was way beyond THEIR ability to pay. They were armed from attacks from their enemy on the outside, but they were feeling the pressures that come from within their soul of the cost to rebuild the wall.

When we come to Chapter 6 verse 5, we see that the people are influenced from the words of outsiders causing them to start forming their own opinions and views of what God called Nehemiah to do. They were ideas and thoughts like "this rebuilding project was not from God, but to build a kingdom for Nehemiah." The workers grouped together to come against him because of their own burden, but they are blaming the situation on Nehemiah. They tried to justify their position by emphasizing that they already had a king and didn't need Nehemiah to be one. They threatened to take matters to the Persian king.

Verse 8-9: *"I replied to him, no such things as you say have been done; you are inventing them out of your own heart and mind. For they all wanted to frighten us, thinking, their hands will be so weak that the work would not get done. But now strengthen my hands!"*

The people that had been called by God begin to make an impact on those outside. Not understanding the ways of God, those in leadership felt threatened by what building this wall might mean to their personal situation and ruler ship. God's people tend to doubt God when natural opposition, which may sound logical, causes insecurity, anxiety, fear, and confusion to the vision that God has given. Again, the "why" questions enter into the mind of the people.

Many people leave what God has called them to do as a result of the conflict and troubles they encounter thinking that in doing so their troubles will leave.

Nehemiah responds by telling the people that the reports are not true. The people must strengthen the weakened areas where doubt and insecurity have tried to penetrate by tightening the armor of God around them.

In verses 15 -16, the wall is finished. *"When all our enemies heard of it, all the nations around us feared and fell far in their own esteem, for they saw that this work was done by our God."*

The wall has now been built. Around the wall there were gates established that was part of the rebuilding of the wall. Each gate had a designated team of people that were assigned for a specific purpose at the gate of which they were to be in charge. Each gate had a unique position for the city's purposes, yet had to work in unity with the other gates to establish strength and power as one wall around the city.

In Chapter 7:1 we read, *"Now when the wall was built and I had set up the doors, and the gatekeepers, singers, and Levites had been appointed..."*

Notice who is watching over the gates: gatekeepers are those who serve; singers are those who lead in praise to God; and Levites are the priests or sons of God. The post watch of the gates was a 24/7 responsibility. In other words, these gates were manned with the armor of God continually by those that had been crucified with Christ. Their life was not their own, but in a position of strategy for the Kingdom of God.

When we go to verse 3, Nehemiah says, *"Let not the gates of Jerusalem be opened until the sun is hot; and while the watchmen are still on guard, let them shut and bar the doors. Appoint guards from the people of Jerusalem, each to his watch (on the wall) and each opposite his own house."*

The word "sun" can be replaced with "SON" in applying these scriptures for us today. This means that there will not be a releasing of the gates until the SON is red hot, or until it is "high noon" when the LIGHT is shining at HIS brightest. It also means that the pressures we incur in the natural realm will be at their hottest point; when we think we can't take it any longer and we are ready to give up or quit whatever God has called us to do.

Those that will be in the city cannot go out, and those on the outside will not be able to come in until God says it is "high noon." We read in this same verse that the guards would take their position on the wall opposite their own house, yet in verse 4 their houses were not yet built! In verse 5 we read that the people that are counted in the city have a genealogy connection to the city which qualified them to be inside the wall.

Let's get this picture: The people that are within the city are there because of being a son or daughter of someone that was connected to the city of God, not because they had years of experience in being a guard; however, they don't yet have a house. Until the gates are opened so their house can be built, they are to establish themselves as a guard on the wall opposite where there house will be. How many times do you think these people went through their days visualizing their dream home within the city walls while they stood guard? How often did they long for the gates to be opened so that they could start building their homes?

These people had already gone through many trials trying to build the wall while dealing with the attacks from their enemies. They were tired. When the wall was finished they were ready to rest, yet God was calling them to come to a place higher, the top of the wall, and guard the place where their house would be in the city, not telling them how long they would have to continue watch. They would know by a sign when things were at their hottest and the sun was at its brightest. When the SON is red hot, everyone will be steaming and sweating uncontrollably. Water will be pouring out of the flesh. It is the trials and tribulations of our life that this experience occurs. Selah.

The gates to the city each had a particular purpose of entering into the city:

Sheep Gate: Those that are migrating in the world needing to be gathered together by the shepherd. This gate is a place of collecting or coming together. They began to collect the sheep.

Fish Gate: The souls of people that have been seeking for the deeper things of God not satisfied with what tradition or denomination has taught. There are numerous squirming souls ready for harvest gathering. God is repairing the migrating and recollecting.

Old Gate: Symbolic of something that has always been in existence. Represents truth that has always existed; but alienated from the lives of the people.

We can go back today through history and find a company of people that God has used to preserve His word and truth as a seed to be carried into the next generation. God's present truth has always been and will always be. There is nothing new with God.

God is collecting the sheep that have gone astray, and the souls that are squirming with the word of God that has always been in them, but because of traditions and doctrines has been hidden except for a few that have carried the genealogy seed which qualifies them to stay within the walls.

Valley Gate: The main entrance in the west wall (West Gate or Jaffa Gate). This gate symbolizes arrogance. In the Old Testament, if there was an ego issue that God needed to deal with, that person was brought into the city through this gate. They had to go down into the valley to find humility before coming up into the city of God. He is bringing about restoration where there was arrogance.

Dung Gate: Represents a heap of rubbish or filth; a sense of scraping. God is drawing the rejects and outsiders of society into the city. Through all the rejection they have experienced, they are finding their true identity with their Heavenly Father as being a child of God. They are finding out that God loves them unconditionally, and that they are wonderfully and fearfully made!

Fountain Gate: The place of the eye; a place that is obvious. The center or display that catches your eye that everything else evolves around. It is supposed to be the Church; however, what should be a display of Christ has been a reproach. The outside world sees the church as a mockery and insult to God. God is restoring the eye or center display so that when others see the church, His body, they will see HIM and be drawn to HIM.

Water Gate: Spring or new beginning which comes from the word sperm. The restoration of the "seed" of the word of God. The restoring of intimacy, childbirth, and multiplication of the word of God as sons of God ready to do the Father's business. The restoration of creating after our own kind that Adam was originally commanded to do by God in Genesis 1: 27-28a:

> *"So God created man in His own image, in the image and likeness of God He created him; male and female He created them. And God blessed them and said to them, be fruitful, multiply, and fill the earth, and subdue it (using all its vast resources in the service of God and man);"*

Horse Gate: Skipping and leaping for joy; the restoration of joy.

Miphkad Gate: Also known as the Muster Gate. The assignment, the mandate, or command. The repairing of the net for recapturing the commandment of God:

Matthew 22: 37-40: *"You shall love the Lord your God with all your heart and with all your soul and with all your mind (intellect). This is the great (most important, principal) and first commandment. And a second is like it; you shall love your neighbor as (you do) yourself. These two commandments sum up and upon them depend all the Law and the Prophets."*

When we come to Chapter 9, Nehemiah tells us how the Israelites came together and separated themselves from all foreigners. They stood and confessed the sins and iniquities of their fathers; read from the Book of the Law of the Lord; and worshipped God by singing praises and lifting up His name.

In verse 8 of this chapter there is a list of "ites" from which the people had been set free. They were released from the following:

- Canaanite: Freedom from being humiliated or belittled.
- Hittite: Freedom from being terrorized.
- Amorite: Freedom from a place of publicity and pride.
- Perizzite: Freedom from rusty; from being separated or in the wilderness.
- Jebusite: Freedom from being trodden.
- Girgashite: Freedom from being trampled and possessed or ruled over.

A very prevalent disease during Bible history was Leprosy which is symbolic of the "disease of the mind." It was a disease that the people were very fearful of being around. Those that had it blamed someone other than themselves for the responsibility of their condition or negative circumstances. Their praises to God included the recollecting of how His people were a "stiff-necked" group complaining constantly, yet God was ready to pardon, gracious and merciful, slow to anger, and of great steadfast love. He did not forsake them and allotted to them the Promised Land (vs. 17, 22).

Something we must consider is; there were those that were called to rebuild the wall; those that were called to guard the gate; those that were called to guard their home; and then those that were princes, Levites, and priests to set the standard for the city. Each of these people were called by God. Chapter 10 gives a list of these people. Their names teach a lesson.

These people had a passion to reestablish the covenant of God and walk in His Law which was given to Moses (vs. 29). They desired to see lost souls come into the city and have a safe place they could reside with their brothers and sisters; This is what all the gates represent.

There is a restoration today calling the people that have labored through this process to bring ALL into the kingdom of God. Each of us has a "gate" that we have come through. Each gate is important and not any greater than another gate. God calls us to come with a spirit of unity and understanding of the importance of the assignment each person has.

We each have a list of "ites" or the Leprosy of our mind that will try to justify why we can't do our portion to what God has called to bring the unity of the family. However, there is a trumpet call that will be heard, and is being heard even now, for each of us to wake up and realize that the purpose of our being is not about us, but about Him. When this happens in each of us; when we experience our "high noon," we will rise up beyond our "ites" to do the Father's business in filling the earth with His glory, setting the captive free and bringing unity to the family of God.

In Revelation Chapter 21: 2-3 we read, *"And I saw the holy city, the new Jerusalem, descending out of heaven from God, all arrayed like a bride beautified and adorned for her husband; Then I heard a mighty voice from the throne and I perceived its distinct words, saying, See! The abode of God is with men, and He will live (encamp, tent) among them; and they shall be His people, and God shall personally be with them and be their God."*

These gates were opened resurrection morning when Jesus Christ rose from the grave for all to come through with whatever situation is going on in our lives. Each gate is separate, yet built of one pearl. (Rev. 21:21). Pearls represent a transformation through trials and tribulations coming through as a stone of righteousness.

"I saw no temple (natural building) in the city (body of Christ), for the Lord God Omnipotent (Himself) and the Lamb (Himself) is its temple. And the city has no need of the sun nor of the moon to give light to it (natural or carnal understanding), for the splendor and radiance (glory) of God illuminate it, and the Lamb is its lamp. The nations (all mankind) shall walk by its light and the rulers and leaders of the earth shall bring into it their glory. And its gates shall never be closed by day, and there shall be no night (sorrow, ignorance) there. They shall bring the glory (the splendor and majesty) and the honor of the nations (our Christ identity) into it." Revelation 21:23-26.

These are they that have moved into place of overcoming by His grace and faith any hindering circumstances and have come a place of higher understanding in God. They know it is not about lifting themselves up, but about establishing their true identity and the unconditional love of God.

"I have been crucified with Christ (in Him I have shared His crucifixion); it is no longer I who live, but Christ (the Messiah) lives in me; and the life I now live in the body I live by faith in (by adherence to and reliance on and complete trust in) the Son of God, who loved me and gave Himself up for me" Galatians 2:20

"In this (union and communion with Him) love is brought to completion and attains perfection with us, that we may have confidence for the Day of Judgment (with assurance and boldness to face Him), because as He is, so are we in this world. There is no fear in love (dread does not exist), but full grown (complete, perfect) love turns fear out of doors and expels every trace of terror! For fear brings with it the thought of punishment and (so) he who is afraid has not reached the full maturity of love (is not yet grown into love's complete perfection). We love Him, because He first loved us." I John 4:17-19.

The Prayer of Jesus Christ

During one of my many quiet times I was having with Father, He told me to read the prayer that Jesus prayer in John 17. After much meditation on these Scriptures, He then told me to use the mind of Christ in me making this prayer my prayer. This opened a whole different realm of understanding my responsibility as a son of God. Afterwards, He told me to share what the Holy Spirit revealed to me. As I was writing I found myself wanting to justify with other Scriptures where this personal implication could be found. Father told me to stop justifying and just to write what His Spirit has revealed. This is wisdom given to those that have ears to hear what the Spirit of God is saying to the sons of God.

John 17:13-26 KJV:

"And now come I (one that is mature in Christ) *to thee* (Father); *and these things I speak* (the power of the word and authority coming from within me that you gave me) *in the world* (ignorance, imagination, and darkness), *that they* (your children) *might have my joy* (manifestation of the fruits of the Holy Spirit) *fulfilled in themselves."*

"I have given them thy word (unconditional love, mercy, forgiveness, and grace); *and the world* (carnal mind) *hath hated them* (natural understanding demands justification), *because they are not of the world* (only God-kind can release the unconditional realm) *even as I* (Son of God) *am not of the world."*

"I pray (intercede) *not that thou* (Father) *shouldest take them* (your children) *out of the world* (separate from ignorance and darkness of a relationship with God as Father), *but that thou* (Father) *shouldest keep*

them (anointed ones, children) *from the evil* (being double-minded with understanding who they are in Christ.)"

"They (mankind) *are not of the world* (antichrist spirit), *even as I* (my life in Christ) *am not of the world* (ignorance to truth)."

"Sanctify (immerse, anoint, cloth) *them through thy truth* (reality that Christ in them is the hope of glory): *thy word* (identifying with the Father's character and nature) *is truth* (as Jesus Christ is, so are we in this world)."

"As thou hast sent me (it was your unconditional love that drew me into understanding that I am your son being equipped to do my Father's business) *into the world* (those that are living in judgment and condemnation), *even so have I* (interceded with unconditional love to all you have brought across my path) *also sent them* (your word will not return void) *into the world* (the ignorance and confusion of who they are)."

"And for their sakes (unity of the body of Christ) *I sanctify* (immerse and cloth holding no man's sins against him) *myself* (Christ identity) *that they also might be sanctified* (walking in Christ identity) *through the truth* (I see all mankind a s born again, sanctified, and righteous because I sit in a heavenly place seeing them as my Father sees the today, even though they may not believe or understand the greatness of His love and mercy that He has bestowed to each person)."

"Neither pray I for these alone (those that have been a direct part of my life), *but for them* (all mankind) *also which shall believe* (every knee will bow and every tongue will confess that Jesus Christ is Lord) *on me* (Christ identity) *through their word* (out of the heart the mouth speaks. Their Christ identity will become real to them.)"

"That they all (mankind) *may be one* (it is the Father's will that no one will perish or else the cross wasn't enough); *as thou, Father, art in me* (I have the DNA of my dad), *and I in thee* (the character and nature),

that they also may be one in us (come to the understanding of their true identity of being a Christ-One with Jesus as the head of the body): *that the world may believe that thou hast sent me* (we have the mind of Christ to be the king, lord, and ambassador for the head of the body; Christ Jesus)."

"And the glory (sonship) *which thou* (Father) *gavest me* (Christ-One) *I have given them* (there is no condemnation in Christ Jesus. I count no man's sins against him); *that they* (those that are brought across my life) *may be one* (come to the understanding of Christ in you), *even as we are one* (the life I now live in the flesh, I live by the faith of the Son of God.)"

"I (Christ-one) *in them* (mankind) *and thou* (identity and character of the Father) *in me* (Christ-one), *that they* (all) *may* (already completed) *be made perfect* (transformed to manifest unconditional love life, and light) *in one* (their true identity in God in one body of Christ); *and that the world* (ignorance and imagination of our natural mind) *may know* (intimacy of covenant exchange) *that thou hast sent me* (Chris-One), *and hast loved them* (unconditionally), *as thou* (Father) *hast loved me* (we are sons of God)."

"Father, I will (my identity in you) *that they* (those that are brought across my path) *also, whom thou hast given me, be with me* (heavenly understanding while in the flesh) *where I am* (mind of Christ) *that they may behold my glory* (doing the Father's business with His authority and power as a son of God), *which thou hast given me* (those I am to disciple): *for thou lovedst me* (unconditionally) *before the foundation of the world* (before time; before ignorance and darkness were created by Adam; before I was conceived in my mother's womb)."

"O righteous Father, the world (natural understanding) *hath not known thee* (your ways of justice*); but I* (Christ-One) *have known thee* (covenant exchange understanding), *and these* (those you have brought

across my path) *have known that thou* (Father) *hast sent me* (I am in this world, but not of it.)"

"And I (Christ-One) *have declared unto them thy name* (you are their Father, creator of all), *and will declare it* (manifesting your character and nature); *that the love* (unconditional) *where with thou* (Father) *hast loved me* (you gave your life) *may be in them* (they have your DNA), *and I* (Christ-one) *in them* (together we are one body of Christ with Jesus as the head.)"

May this prayer be heard and understood with the mind of Christ and the wisdom of God.

About the Author

Bishop Audrey Drummonds is the founder and director of Interior Coverings Ministry and Outreach Missions in Groveland, Florida, since 2002. She has a PhD in religious philosophy and master's of divinity from Tabernacle Bible College and Seminary, with a bachelor's from Liberty University. She is the presiding bishop of the World Communion of Christian Celtic Convergence Churches into the USA. Ministry has taken her into over forty countries, including, Israel, Greece, Turkey, Peru, India, Kenya, Philippines, India, Canada, England, Mexico, Honduras, and Russia. She writes, lectures, teaches, and speaks for Interior Coverings Ministry and the WCCC. She resides with her husband in Florida.

Printed in the United States
by Baker & Taylor Publisher Services